PARENT-TEACHER COLLECTION

Multi-Grade Readers Theatre

**Recent titles in Teacher Ideas Press
Readers Theatre Series**

Around the World Through Holidays: Cross Curricular Readers Theatre
Written and Illustrated by Carol Peterson

Wings of Fancy: Using Readers Theatre to Study the Fantasy Genre
Joan Garner

Nonfiction Readers Theatre for Beginning Readers
Anthony D. Fredericks

Mother Goose Readers Theatre for Beginning Readers
Anthony D. Fredericks

MORE Frantic Frogs and Other Frankly Fractured Folktales for Readers Theatre
Anthony D. Fredericks

Songs and Rhymes Readers Theatre for Beginning Readers
Anthony D. Fredericks

Readers Theatre for Middle School Boys: Investigating the Strange and Mysterious
Ann N. Black

African Legends, Myths, and Folktales for Readers Theatre
Anthony D. Fredericks

Against All Odds: Readers Theatre for Grades 3–8
Suzanne I. Barchers and Michael Ruscoe

Readers Theatre for African American History
Jeff Sanders and Nancy I. Sanders

Building Fluency with Readers Theatre: Motivational Strategies, Successful Lessons, and
Dynamic Scripts to Develop Fluency, Comprehension, Writing, and Vocabulary
Anthony D. Fredericks

American Folklore, Legends, and Tall Tales for Readers Theatre
Anthony D. Fredericks

Multi-Grade Readers Theatre

Picture Book Authors and Illustrators

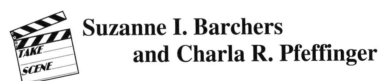 **Suzanne I. Barchers
and Charla R. Pfeffinger**

Readers Theatre

A Teacher Ideas Press Book

Libraries Unlimited
An Imprint of ABC-CLIO, LLC

A B C ❖ C L I O

Santa Barbara, California • Denver, Colorado • Oxford, England

Library of Congress Cataloging-in-Publication Data

Barchers, Suzanne I.
    Multi-grade readers theatre : picture book authors and illustrators / Suzanne I. Barchers and
  Charla R. Pfeffinger.
      p. cm. — (Readers theatre)
   Includes index.
    ISBN 978-1-59158-819-1 (pbk : alk. paper) — ISBN 978-1-59158-821-4 (ebook) 1. Oral reading.
  2. Readers' theater. 3. Picture books for children. I. Pfeffinger, Charla R. II. Title.
   LB1573.5.B373 2009
   372.45'2—dc22   2009011981

13   12   11   10   9   1   2   3   4   5

This book is also available on the World Wide Web as an eBook.
Visit www.abc-clio.com for details.

ABC-CLIO, LLC
130 Cremona Drive, P.O. Box 1911
Santa Barbara, California 93116-1911

This book is printed on acid-free paper ∞
Manufactured in the United States of America

For Bob, my best friend, best support, and best love.
—SIB

For my husband Lyle, who has always encouraged me to be the best I can be.
He has walked through the valleys of my life and stood on the mountaintops
with me for twenty-eight years.
—CRP

Contents

**Part Two:
Grades Two, Three, and Four**

Introduction

From Verna Aardema to Margot Zemach, talented authors and illustrators of picture books have been dedicated to ensuring that their work will appeal to generations of children. The scripts in *Multi-Grade Readers Theatre: Picture Book Authors and Illustrators* provide students with a snapshot of the lives of thirty-six well-known authors, illustrators, and poets. Drawn from biographies, autobiographies, interviews, news articles, obituaries, and Internet sources, the essential facts of each person's story have been carefully researched. The conversations, however, are largely fictional. In some cases, the script is fanciful, and the readers learn about the author or illustrator through book characters, such as the ducks in Robert McCloskey's *Make Way for Ducklings*.

There are thirty-six scripts, allowing for a weekly script during the school year. These short scripts are intended to be introduced, read, and discussed in a thirty-minute class period. The scripts are further developed to accommodate a minimum of three grade levels. These levels, indicated on the introductory page, may be disclosed to the students at your discretion. Thereby, a librarian or teacher can assign parts to accommodate three grade levels within a class.

Each script has been evaluated using the Flesch-Kincaid readability formula for grade level. Once the proper nouns have been eliminated, the scripts have a readability level of grades one, two, and three in the first half of the book. The second half of the book encompasses grades two, three, and four. There are a few scripts with broader grade levels because of the inclusion of poetry or nursery rhymes. Some scripts have lines spoken by *Everyone* or *Audience,* allowing the inclusion of all students. With the varying grade levels and the predictability of these scripts, they are particularly well suited for remedial readers.

Using Readers Theatre

Readers theatre can be compared to radio plays. The emphasis is on an effective reading of the script rather than on a dramatic, memorized presentation. Reading orally helps develops strong reading skills, and listening to scripts promotes active listening for students in the audience. Paraphrasing of the lines, a natural happenstance, should be allowed. Challenging names of characters and places may be written on the board and rehearsed in advance. In some scripts, the narrators have more difficult passages, and they should rehearse their lines carefully. If time allows, all students should have ample opportunity to familiarize themselves with their lines.

Preparing the Scripts

Once scripts are chosen for reading, make enough copies for each character, plus an extra set or two for your use and a replacement copy. To help readers keep their place, have students use highlighter markers to designate their character's role within the copy. For example, someone reading the role of Narrator 1 could highlight the lines in blue, with another character highlighting the lines in yellow.

Photocopied scripts will last longer if you use a three-hole punch (or copy them on pre-punched paper) and place them in inexpensive folders. The folders can be color-coordinated to the internal highlighting for each character's part. The title of the play can be printed on the outside of the folder, and scripts can be easily stored for the next reading. The preparation of the scripts is a good project for a student aide or volunteer parent. The preparation takes a minimum of initial attention and needs to be repeated only when a folder is lost.

Getting Started

For the first experience with a readers theatre script, choose a script with many characters to involve more students. Gather the students informally. Introduce readers theatre by explaining that readers theatre does not mean memorizing a play and acting it out, but rather reading a script aloud with perhaps a few props and actions. If possible, have the students listen to some radio plays, which can be found on several Internet sites.

If readability levels are not an issue for your students, allow volunteers to do an initial reading of a script, providing an opportunity to review their parts before reading aloud. If preferred, assign the parts according to the reading levels of your students. Write pronunciations of any challenging names or words on the board. While one group of students is preparing to read a script, another group could be reviewing a different script, brainstorming ideas for staging and props, or reading books by the author or illustrator who is the subject of the script.

Presentation Suggestions

For readers theatre, readers traditionally stand—or sit on stools, chairs, or the floor—in a formal presentation style. The narrators may stand with the script placed on music stands or lecterns slightly off to one or both sides. The readers may hold their scripts in black or colored folders. The position of the reader indicates the importance of the role. On occasion, key characters might sit on high stools to elevate them above numerous other characters. The scripts include a few suggestions for presentation, but students should be encouraged to create interesting arrangements.

Props

Readers theatre has no, or few, props. However, if time allows, simple costuming effects will lend interest to the presentation. Students should be encouraged to decide how much or little to add to their reading. For some readers, the use of props or actions may be distracting, and the emphasis should remain on the reading rather than on an overly complicated presentation.

Delivery Suggestions

Delivery suggestions generally are not imbedded in the scripts. Therefore, it is important to discuss with the students what will make the scripts come alive as they read. During their first experiences with presenting a script, students are tempted to keep their heads buried in the script, making sure they don't miss a line. Students should learn the material well enough to look up from the script during the presentation. Students can learn to use onstage focus—to look at each other during the presentation. This is most logical for characters who are interacting with each other. The use of offstage focus—the presenters look directly into the eyes of the audience—is more logical for the narrator or characters who are uninvolved with onstage characters. Alternatively, have students who do not interact with each other focus on a prearranged offstage location, such as the classroom clock, during delivery. Simple actions can also be incorporated into readers theatre.

Generally the audience should be able to see the readers' facial expressions during the reading. On occasion, it might seem logical for a character to move across the stage, facing the other characters while reading. In this event, the characters should be turned enough so that the audience can see the reader's face.

The Next Step

The scripts provide an opportunity for preparing a special program or for a diversion from the regular curriculum. A readers theatre workshop could be held periodically, with each student belonging to a group that prepares a script for presentation. A readers theatre festival could be planned for a special day when several short scripts are presented consecutively, with brief intermissions between each reading. Consider grouping together related scripts. For example, scripts about illustrators who have won the Caldecott Medal could be presented after the script about Randolph Caldecott.

Students who are particularly inspired by the stories they have read in this collection of scripts should be encouraged to do further reading about these and other authors and illustrators of picture books. Once students have enjoyed the reading process involved in preparing and presenting readers theatre, they can create their own scripts. All of the subjects of this book are no longer living, providing students with many possibilities for writing scripts about their favorite living authors and illustrators.

Part One

Grades One, Two, and Three

Why Mosquitoes Buzz in People's Ears

Verna Aardema

1911–2000

Summary and Background Information

Verna Aardema wrote many books based on folktales from Mexico and Africa. She would tell them to her daughter and write the tales down for publication. In this script, the readers focus on *Why Mosquitoes Buzz in People's Ears*. Illustrated by Leo and Diane Dillon, the book received the Caldecott Medal in 1976 and the Brooklyn Art Books for Children Award in 1977. This script alludes to the theme of the book, which is that it is better to listen carefully. In the script, the girls can't hear what they boys are buzzing about, in part because they don't want to listen. They finally cause the boys to leave after the boys are reminded of the events in the Aardema story.

Presentation Suggestions

The narrator should sit to one side of the room after introducing the setting and return to the center during the conclusion of the script. Actions imbedded in the script should be followed by the readers. The script is designed to involve the whole class, not just the characters who present it. The girls and boys should get more and more insistent with their various responses during the script. Prepare the following cue cards: BOYS: Buzz, buzz, buzz; GIRLS: Go away! Go away!; GIRLS: Hurray! Hurray!

Introductory and Follow-up Suggestions

Show students where Africa and Mexico are on a map. Then ask:

- In every family there are stories that we tell each other year after year. This is true in other countries also. Some of these stories are never written down. Verna Aardema loved to hear these stories from Mexico and Africa and would tell them to her daughter. Do you know what these stories are called? (Folktales)

- Why do you think people tell folktales?

After reading the script, discuss how Verna Aardema chose to write this story. Then ask:

- Is it better to write down a folktale or to tell it over and over?

- Do your grandparents tell you stories about their lives when they were young? These stories are called oral histories. Why should they be written down?

Characters

Grade One: Boys, Garth, Heidi, Tanya, Buck, Wendy

Grade Two: Narrator, Jenell, Girls, Connie, Sophie, Luke, Sadie, Bruce, Mari

Grade Three: Mr. Bright, Wendell

Why Mosquitoes Buzz in People's Ears

Narrator: Mr. Bright has asked his students to form five groups. Each group is to read a book and then write a skit about it. They have had a week to practice their skits, and now it is time to present their skits to the class.

Mr. Bright: Today each group will present its script, so I hope you are prepared.

Wendell: Mr. Bright, my group is ready to present our skit. May we go first?

Mr. Bright: Sure, Wendell. Class, let's pay attention as Wendell's group does its skit.

Wendell: Before we begin, I need to explain how you are all going to be part of our skit. When Jenell holds up this card, the girls will say, "Go away! Go away!" *(Jenell holds up her card.)* When Sadie holds up this card, girls will say, "Hurray! Hurray!" *(Sadie holds up her card.)* When Buck holds up this card, boys will all say, "Buzz, buzz, buzz." *(Buck holds up his card.)* Ready?

Jenell: You forgot the hand swats.

Wendell: Oh, yes. Girls, you should swat the air around your ears when you say, "Go away! Go away!" Let's start our skit.

(Buck holds up his card. Repeat as appropriate throughout script.)

Boys: Buzz, buzz, buzz.

(Jenell holds up her card. Repeat as appropriate throughout script.)

Girls: Go away! Go away!

Boys: Buzz, buzz, buzz.

Girls: Go away! Go away!

Connie: Didn't you hear us say go away?

From *Multi-Grade Readers Theatre: Picture Book Authors and Illustrators* by Suzanne I. Barchers and Charla R. Pfeffinger. Santa Barbara, CA: Teacher Ideas Press/Libraries Unlimited. Copyright © 2009.

Garth: This is how we prefer to spend our day.

Boys: Buzz, buzz, buzz.

Sophie: You're such pests. Why must you stay?

Girls: Go away! Go away!

Garth: We like to buzz around your head.

Boys: Buzz, buzz, buzz.

Heidi: We don't like to hear that buzz. Find someone else instead!

Tanya: Who are you that you buzz and buzz?

Luke: We're mosquitoes. When we say, buzz, buzz, buzz, what do you hear?

Boys: Buzz, buzz, buzz.

Sadie: We hear nothing! You just make annoying noise.

Sophie: No wonder you are such pests!

Boys: Buzz, buzz, buzz.

Girls: Go away! Go away!

Bruce: Silly girls, you need to know what we have to say.

Jenell: Sadie told you, you say nothing, that's what you say!

Buck: You are wrong, you know. We don't just buzz to waste the day. We do have something to say.

Mari: If you do have something to say, we don't get it so . . .

Girls: Go away! Go away!

Boys: Buzz, buzz, buzz.

Jenell: Won't you please just . . .

Girls: Go away! Go away!

Wendell: If you can't hear what we have to say, I guess we should go away.

Girls: Hurray! Hurray!

Garth: Do we really have to go? *(All the girls nod their heads yes.)* Then before we go, I want a bite.

From *Multi-Grade Readers Theatre: Picture Book Authors and Illustrators* by Suzanne I. Barchers and Charla R. Pfeffinger. Santa Barbara, CA: Teacher Ideas Press/Libraries Unlimited. Copyright © 2009.

Heidi: Now that's just not right!

Boys: Buzz, buzz, buzz.

Sadie: What are you buzz buzzing about?

Luke: If you won't hear what we have to say, we'll have a bite and be on our way.

Wendy: If you bite, we will fight. You know who will lose if there is a fight. So . . .

Girls: Go away! Go away!

Buck: Oh, come on girls, you can't fight us. We're too quick for you.

Bruce: Even with very fast hands, you're not as fast as me. You can't beat any of us.

Boys: Buzz, buzz, buzz.

Mari: Boys, you know you're wrong. I know we can defeat you.

Sophie: Let's put you to the test and see who really is the best. Or just . . .

Girls: Go away! Go away!

Wendell: Boys, we really do have important things to say. These girls, they just don't hear us. I think it's time we leave this place and find someone who will listen.

(Sadie holds up her card.)

Girls: Hurray! Hurray!

Boys: Buzz, buzz, buzz.

Wendell: Before we mosquitoes go away, I want to ask a question. Why do mosquitoes buzz in people's ears?

Connie: Because you are pests. Just like in the book *Why Do Mosquitoes Buzz in People's Ears?*

Sadie: You buzz and tell silly stories. Even the iguana didn't want to hear you. He put sticks in his ears and then he couldn't hear anyone.

From *Multi-Grade Readers Theatre: Picture Book Authors and Illustrators* by Suzanne I. Barchers and Charla R. Pfeffinger. Santa Barbara, CA: Teacher Ideas Press/Libraries Unlimited. Copyright © 2009.

Mari: Then things just went crazy in the story. All because you . . .

Boys: Buzz, buzz, buzz.

Connie: Right. So why don't you just . . .

Girls: Go away! Go away!

Garth: All right, we will. But you'll never know what we had to say. Come on boys.

Boys: Buzz, buzz, buzz.

Mr. Bright: Very well done. I know most of you have read the book *Why Do Mosquitoes Buzz in People's Ears?* Can anyone tell me how the story came about?

Bruce: It is an African folk story. Mrs. Aardema told it to her little girl. Then she put it into a book.

Mr. Bright: That's right. Now, I'm afraid we are out of time. So if you are wondering how the story ends, you'll have to read the book. Buzz away . . . buzz away . . . but come back after lunch! We'll have the next skit.

A Writing Pioneer

Margaret Wise Brown
1910–1952

Summary and Background Information

Margaret Wise Brown wrote numerous books and stories during her life. She is best known for *Goodnight Moon!* and *Runaway Bunny*. She spent many hours listening to children tell their stories and enjoying the poetry they wrote while she was at the Bank Street Experimental School in New York City. That was how she learned to write in a vocabulary and rhythm that appeal to children. She drew on her love of animals as she created main characters for her books. She also used the everyday things in a child's world to write about. She was passionate about her books, her life, and the rights of those artists who worked with her. Unfortunately, she died at age forty-two while in Europe.

Presentation Suggestions

This is a two-part script. The narrators should sit to one side of the staging area at all times. Part one is the dialogue with a role for children to read or respond to in unison. A few children or the rest of the class can read these lines. If you elect to have the whole class read in this role, consider making cue cards with the narrators cueing the class for their responses. Ms. Jackson and the narrators can be seated in chairs.

Introductory and Follow-up Suggestions

Before reading the script, read aloud *Goodnight Moon!* Then ask:

- What do you know about Margaret Wise Brown?
- What do you think it means to be paid a "royalty" for writing a book?

After reading the script, ask:

- How would you keep your food fresh if you had no electricity?

- How would you stay warm if you had no furnace?

- Calling someone a bird brain these days is not considered polite. Why do you think Margaret Wise Brown named their group such a name?

Share additional books by Margaret Wise Brown with the students.

Characters

Grade One: Esther, Children, Isabel

Grade Two: Narrator Two, Bernie, Jeremy, Vicky, Gabriel, Owen, Will

Grade Three: Narrator One, Ms. Jackson

A Writing Pioneer

Narrator One: The summer book clubs meet each Tuesday. A group of older readers helps Ms. Jackson with the younger ones.

Narrator Two: The five year olds have a list of books their parents may read to them. On the list is *Goodnight Moon!* The older readers ask the children about the book.

Esther: What book begins with "In the green, green room"?

Children: *Goodnight Moon!*

Bernie: What is hanging from the ceiling?

Children: A big red balloon.

Jeremy: Who sleeps in the green room?

Children: A bunny.

Isabel: What does the bunny tell each thing in the room?

Children: Goodnight.

Vicky: Why does the room get darker and darker?

Children: The moon goes away.

Gabriel: Do you see any pictures on the wall?

Children: Yes.

Esther: What is the cow doing in the picture?

Children: It's jumping over the moon.

Bernie: How does the bunny tell what time it is when he is in his room?

Children: There is a clock in his room.

Isabel: What else is in the bunny's room?

Children: A mouse is in the room. Kittens are in the room.

Jeremy: What is the last thing the bunny says in the book?

Children: Goodnight Moon.

Ms. Jackson: Can you tell our friends thank you for being here with us today?

Children: Thank you.

Narrator One: It is time for the little ones to leave. The older readers stay with Ms. Jackson.

Ms. Jackson: I hope that you enjoyed your time with the children. I want to tell you about the author of that book. Margaret Wise Brown wrote *Goodnight Moon!* She wrote many other children's books.

Owen: How did she begin writing books?

Ms. Jackson: She would spend a lot of time talking to children. She would listen to them as they made up stories and poems. She used the way they talked to help her write her stories and poems. She was a pioneer in the field of writing for children.

Vicky: What do you mean by a pioneer?

Ms. Jackson: She was one of the first writers to write books just for children.

Esther: What did kids read before that?

Ms. Jackson: There were fairy tales. And there were fables. Because she was an unusual person, she liked her writing to be unusual, too.

Will: Why do you say she was unusual?

Ms. Jackson: She liked to play practical jokes on people. She had a house in New York. She called it Cobble Court. She tied cherries or lemons to a potted tree in her yard. She wanted to fool city folk into thinking she had an unusually skillful green thumb.

Isabel: It sounds like she really enjoyed having fun. What else did she do?

From *Multi-Grade Readers Theatre: Picture Book Authors and Illustrators* by Suzanne I. Barchers and Charla R. Pfeffinger. Santa Barbara, CA: Teacher Ideas Press/Libraries Unlimited. Copyright © 2009.

Ms. Jackson: There were no utilities such as electricity in her house. She covered the floors, walls, and furniture with fur. She kept her house warm with fires in a fireplace. She used her well as a refrigerator. She would hang things from a rope to keep them cold. She also had a house in Maine. She called it The Only House.

Owen: Ms. Jackson, that's crazy. Are you making this up?

Ms. Jackson: No, I told you she was unusual. She had a lot of friends. They started the *Bird Brain Society.*

Gabriel: What did their society do?

Ms. Jackson: Any one of them could say it was Christmas Day. They would all stop everything and have Christmas.

Bernie: I think I like that club. Christmas every day! That's a great idea.

Ms. Jackson: It does sound like fun, doesn't it? She wasn't all fun and games, however. She was very serious about her work. The artists that illustrated her books didn't get paid very well. She demanded that they get royalties, just like she did.

Jeremy: What do you mean by royalties?

Ms. Jackson: A royalty is a percent of the price of a book. The more books that sell, the more money she'd make. Ms. Brown's books sold very well, so she made a lot of money. She wanted the artists who worked on her books to make a lot of money, too.

Isabel: I bet she got her way, didn't she?

Ms. Jackson: Yes, she did. She was very strict with the artists that worked with her, too. She set deadlines and expected everyone to keep them.

Will: I bet you know a story about that too, don't you?

Ms. Jackson: There was one artist who was not working fast enough. They were doing a book with Kerry Blue dogs as the characters. She bought two puppies to be his models. After a long day of painting pictures for the books, the artist took a nap. When he woke up, the puppies had licked all of the paint off of the pictures.

Esther: I bet they were both mad at those puppies!

Ms. Jackson: I think you are probably right. Ms. Brown was the first writer to do a series of books. They were called the "Noisy Books." Who can tell me why?

Gabriel: The books were about things around us that make noise.

Ms. Jackson: That's right. She wanted the readers to listen to what was around them. She wrote with the idea that children would like to read about their own world. And she knew that that world could be a lot of fun.

Narrator Two: Ms. Brown turned her dreams into words that could make a child laugh. Her words could make a child's life fun, even on a bad day. They still do.

From *Multi-Grade Readers Theatre: Picture Book Authors and Illustrators* by Suzanne I. Barchers and Charla R. Pfeffinger. Santa Barbara, CA: Teacher Ideas Press/Libraries Unlimited. Copyright © 2009.

A Beautiful World

Barbara Cooney

1917–2005

Summary and Background Information

Barbara Cooney started as an illustrator for books when she realized her art history degree was not going to provide a living. Her work was derailed when she entered the Women's Army Corps during World War II. She eventually married and had two children. After a divorce, she resumed illustrating to provide for her and her two children. She later remarried and had two more children. She traveled extensively, and after becoming a widow, she moved to Colorado until her death. Her book, *Miss Rumphius,* won the Caldecott Medal. Although she said the book was not really about her, there is a strong story line that parallels her life, although she did not retire by the sea. This script starts with a conversation between Barbara and a friend and then shifts to a classroom story time to discuss the book *Miss Rumphius.*

Presentation Suggestions

Arrange the readers in the following order: Narrator, Barbara Cooney, Sarah Hayes, Ellen Hayes, and the remaining readers. The student readers can be seated on the floor, with the other readers in chairs. Place a copy of *Miss Rumphius* in view.

Introductory and Follow-up Suggestions

Describe where you spent your summers when growing up. Then ask:

- Do any of you visit your grandparents or other relatives during summer vacation?

- What makes visiting relatives special?

After reading the script, ask:

- Do you like the area where you live—the environment, the climate, and so forth? Why or why not?

• Miss Rumphis worked to make her community better. What could we do to improve our schoolyard (community, neighborhood, park, etc.)?

List on the board a variety of things children can do to make the world more beautiful. This could include easy projects around the school ground such as picking up the trash or planting seeds for a flower garden. Organize the projects from easy to hard, inexpensive to expensive. Encourage the students to commit to a project individually or in groups.

Characters

Grade One: Sarah Hayes, Benny

Grade Two: Barbara Cooney, Ellen Hayes, Judy, George, Fanny, Courtney, Peter

Grade Three: Narrator, Cathy

A Beautiful World

Narrator: Barbara Cooney is having tea with a friend. She talks about what it was like to grow up in the city.

Barbara Cooney: When I was a child, we lived in the suburbs of Brooklyn, New York. I hated city life. My favorite days were when I was sick.

Sarah Hayes: Why did you like being sick?

Barbara Cooney: I could stay home from school and draw all day. I loved to draw. My grandmother is the one who helped me learn to love drawing. She was an amateur painter.

Sarah Hayes: Where did she live?

Barbara Cooney: She lived in Maine, in the country. I would spend summers there, and it was just wonderful. I loved being away from the suburbs and all of the noise. The countryside was so peaceful. And my grandmother gave me the freedom to learn how to paint.

Sarah Hayes: How did she do that?

Barbara Cooney: She let me use her paints all I wanted. I did have one rule, however. I had to keep my brushes clean. I wish I had gone to art school.

Sarah Hayes: Why didn't you?

Barbara Cooney: I don't know. I did go to Smith College. I studied art history there. Now that I use art for my books, art school would have been a better choice.

Sarah Hayes: Have you always worked on books?

Barbara Cooney: No. During World War II, I joined the Women's Army Corps. While in the army, I got married. I left the service when I had my daughter, Gretel. My husband and I bought a farm. In the summer, we had camps for children. Then I had my son, Barnaby. I was divorced and later married again. I had two more children, Charles and Phoebe Ann.

From *Multi-Grade Readers Theatre: Picture Book Authors and Illustrators* by Suzanne I. Barchers and Charla R. Pfeffinger. Santa Barbara, CA: Teacher Ideas Press/Libraries Unlimited. Copyright © 2009.

Sarah Hayes: Of all of your books, which is your favorite?

Barbara Cooney: I don't know that I have a favorite. *Miss Rumphius* is one I love. She is like me in some ways. She travels all over the world and then she lives in the country when she is older.

Sarah Hayes: I can see why you like the book . . . . Oh, dear. Look at the time. I need to stop by the school. I'm meeting my sister after her class.

Barbara Cooney: It's time for me to go, too. Let's get together again soon! I'll buy the tea next time!

Narrator: Sarah Hayes goes into her sister's classroom. Ellen Hayes has just read *Miss Rumphius* to the class. She motions for Sarah to take a seat.

Ellen Hayes: Let's talk about the book. What did Miss Alice Rumphius want to do?

Cathy: She wanted to make the world more beautiful.

Ellen Hayes: Who told her to make the world more beautiful?

Cathy: Her grandfather told her.

Ellen Hayes: Did she do that first or later in her life, Benny?

Benny: No, first she worked in a library. She dusted the books.

Ellen Hayes: What else did she do at the library?

Judy: She helped people find books to read. And she read a lot of books about faraway places.

George: She thought it would be fun to go to those faraway places. So she traveled a lot.

Ellen Hayes: Do you remember where she went?

Fanny: She went to an island. There were monkeys and cockatoos there.

George: And she met a king! His name was Bapa Raja.

Courtney: When it was time for her to leave the island, the king gave her a special seashell. It had a bird drawn on it. The words, "You'll always be in my heart" were on it, too.

From *Multi-Grade Readers Theatre: Picture Book Authors and Illustrators* by Suzanne I. Barchers and Charla R. Pfeffinger. Santa Barbara, CA: Teacher Ideas Press/Libraries Unlimited. Copyright © 2009.

Ellen Hayes: Where else did she go?

Peter: She climbed up huge mountains! Then she went into the deserts and the jungles. She sure was brave to do so much!

Ellen Hayes: She did get to do a lot, didn't she? Where did she go after her trips?

Benny: Back to live by the sea in the country. That was where she liked it best.

Sarah Hayes: Excuse me. Can I tell you something I just learned?

Ellen Hayes: Of course you can. Is it something about *Miss Rumphius*?

Sarah Hayes: It is about the author. I just had tea with Barbara Cooney. She is a friend of mine.

Judy: Did she talk about how she came to write this story? Does she look like Miss Rumphius?

Sarah Hayes: She talked a lot about what it was like to grow up. And I think you are right. She looks a bit like Miss Rumphius!

Peter: Did she live in the city or in the country?

Sarah Hayes: She lived in the city. She spent her summers in the country with her grandmother. She taught Mrs. Cooney to love to draw.

Fanny: She sounds a lot like Miss Rumphius. She had a special person who taught her things.

Cathy: Did Barbara Cooney travel a lot too?

Sarah Hayes: Yes, she did. She was also in the army during World War II. And she had four kids! But I don't think she planted lupine seeds. And, like us, she lives by the mountains, not by the sea.

Courtney: I think she gave us something special with her books. Those live on, just like flowers.

George: They make the world more beautiful.

Sarah Hayes: That is so true.

Ellen Hayes: Do you think she would come to visit us some day? Perhaps we could talk about how to make our school more beautiful.

Sarah Hayes: I will ask her the next time we have tea. I think she would like the idea of helping you.

Ellen Hayes: Time to go home!

Narrator: The students leave Ellen Hayes's classroom. Ellen turns to her sister.

Ellen Hayes: Do you *really* know Barbara Cooney?

Sarah Hayes: Now, Ellen, have I ever lied to you? Let's go have tea! I think I'll have a scone with mine. How about you? Maybe I'll tell you who I ran into at breakfast.

From *Multi-Grade Readers Theatre: Picture Book Authors and Illustrators* by Suzanne I. Barchers and Charla R. Pfeffinger. Santa Barbara, CA: Teacher Ideas Press/Libraries Unlimited. Copyright © 2009.

A Most Famous Elephant

Jean de Brunhoff

1899–1937

Summary and Background Information

Jean de Brunhoff was born in Paris. He joined the French army at the end of World War I and reached the front lines when the war was nearly over. Returning to Paris, he decided to become a professional artist and he studied painting. In 1924, de Brunhoff married Cecile Sabourand, and the couple had three sons: Laurent, Mathieu, and Thierry. In 1930, Cecile de Brunhoff invented a bedtime story about a little elephant to amuse their four year old, Mathieu, who was ill. Jean wrote the story as it was retold to him by his son. In 1931, it was published as *Histoire de Babar, le petit éléphant*. In 1933, the story was published in English. *The Story of Babar, the Little Elephant* became the springboard for a series of Babar books, first written by Jean and then by his son Laurent after Jean died.

Presentation Suggestions

The narrator and readers should all sit in a semicircle so they can see each other and the listening audience as they interact while they read.

Introductory and Follow-up Suggestions

Before reading the script, discuss how people learn lessons from all sorts of places: from their parents, their friends, their teachers, and so forth. Then ask:

- Writers use animals to tell a story that has a lesson for people to learn. Why do you think they use animals?

- Do you have a favorite book about an animal?

21

- How many elephants can you name that are in storybooks?

After reading the script, discuss how Jean and Laurent de Brunhoff wrote a series of books. Then ask:

- What is the name of the series of books about a monkey? (*Curious George* by H. A. Rey)

- What do we mean by a "series" of books?

- What is your favorite series?

Characters

Grade One: Baby Elephant One, Baby Elephant Two, Mama Elephant, Marsha

Grade Two: Narrator One, Narrator Two, Mr. Perry, Ahmed, Denise, Mason, Callie, Carlos, Hayden

Grade Three: Papa Elephant, Uncle Elephant, Janey, Jocelyn

A Most Famous Elephant

Narrator One: A small herd of elephants lives in a big zoo. The young ones dream of being famous one day. Today they talk with each other about life at the zoo.

Baby Elephant One: Look at all the people watching us. They must think we are special.

Mama Elephant: You are very special to me. The kids love to watch you.

Baby Elephant Two: That's just because we're in a zoo. I wish we were famous. Do you know any famous elephants?

Papa Elephant: There are many famous elephants. Jumbo was in the Paris and London zoos for a while. Then he was in a circus.

Mama Elephant: He was a hero, too. He saved a baby elephant from being hit by a train. But he was hit and died.

Papa Elephant: Queenie lived in Australia. She was very smart and gave kids rides on her back. She could also be naughty. If the kids teased her, sometimes she squirted them with water!

Uncle Elephant: These days the most famous elephants are not real. They are in movies or cartoons or books. One even flies, if you can imagine that!

Baby Elephant One: How do you find out about them?

Uncle Elephant: I listen to the school children that visit. Look, here comes a group now. They always seem to be talking about elephants. Let's listen to this group.

Mr. Perry: I just love elephants, don't you? They are so big and strong, and I love the way their trunks sway back and forth as they run.

Janey: I love books about elephants. My favorite is the story about Babar. Ahmed and I did a report on the de Brunhoffs last year. They started the series of books.

From *Multi-Grade Readers Theatre: Picture Book Authors and Illustrators* by Suzanne I. Barchers and Charla R. Pfeffinger. Santa Barbara, CA: Teacher Ideas Press/Libraries Unlimited. Copyright © 2009.

Mr. Perry: There is a good story about the authors. What can you tell us about it, Ahmed?

Ahmed: Cecile de Brunhoff, a young mother, made up Babar. Her four-year-old son was sick. She told him the Babar story at bedtime. The story made him feel better.

Mr. Perry: That's right. Later, Cecile's sons told their father the story. He wrote it down, and then he drew the pictures. His name was Jean de Brunhoff. The book was first published in French. Then it came out in English and was called *The Story of Babar, the Little Elephant.*

Denise: I have read a lot of the Babar books, but some don't have Jean de Brunhoff's name on the cover of the book. They say Laurent de Brunhoff. I don't understand that. Who is Laurent?

Ahmed: I can explain that. When Jean was a young man, he became very ill. He had tuberculosis. The doctors said he could not stay home. So while he was away, he wrote five more stories for his sons.

Mason: But I am sure I have read more than six Babar books. How many Babar books did Jean write once he was well?

Ahmed: Jean wrote six Babar books before he died. His oldest son wrote the other fifty Babar books. His name was Laurent. That is why some books have a different first name.

Jocelyn: What was the last book that Jean wrote?

Janey: It was *Babar and Father Christmas.* His other books were *The Travels of Babar, ABC of Babar, Zephir's Holidays,* and *Babar and His Family.*

Mason: Did Jean ever get to go back home?

Mr. Perry: No, he didn't. Sadly, he died when he was thirty-seven years old. But his sons knew he loved them because of the books he wrote. He wanted to tell them things they needed to remember when they grew up.

Callie: What did he want them to remember?

Janey: I think he wanted them to remember that you have to work hard in life. When you work hard, people will respect you for it. Also, you need to make other people happy and do the right things, even when that is hard to do.

Carlos: Those are good things to learn.

Marsha: Jean died young just like Babar's mother. His sons must have been just as sad.

Mr. Perry: It is always sad to lose someone you love.

Hayden: At least they didn't need to run away like Babar did.

Marsha: I have seen some of the Babar books on TV. I think it's fun to watch them.

Callie: I like to read the books. Then you can imagine more about the story.

Carlos: Laurent must have liked to imagine things. He wrote a lot more Babar books!

Jocelyn: I really like his books with the bright colors. They show a lot of imagination.

Marsha: Denise, you said you've read a lot of the Babar books. Have you read all fifty of them?

Denise: I don't think so. I should have kept a list, and then I'd know how many I have read.

Mr. Perry: What do you like best about the Babar books, Denise?

Denise: I think Babar is smart and cares about his friends.

Hayden: That's just what Jean wanted his sons to learn from his books.

Janey: Those are the things we *all* should learn from his books. I'm glad Laurent decided to write more books after his father died.

From *Multi-Grade Readers Theatre: Picture Book Authors and Illustrators* by Suzanne I. Barchers and Charla R. Pfeffinger. Santa Barbara, CA: Teacher Ideas Press/Libraries Unlimited. Copyright © 2009.

Marsha: And I am glad they are on TV. Some little kids can't read yet. But they can learn about Babar and then they can read the books.

Mr. Perry: We need to go see the monkeys, class. Anyone know the name of a famous monkey?

Children: I do! I do!

Narrator Two: The elephants watch the class leave to see the monkeys. Then they talk about what they heard.

Baby Elephant Two: Papa, had you heard about Babar before?

Papa Elephant: No, but I know about him and the authors now. I am curious about that famous monkey. Anyone know who he is?

Mama Elephant: Oh, Uncle and I know all about him. Do you want to tell the story?

Uncle Elephant: Let me see what I can remember. Once upon a time there was a man with a yellow hat who went to Africa . . . .

Narrator One: Do you know who that famous monkey is? If you don't, it's time to go to the library. You'll find out what lessons you can learn from those books!

From *Multi-Grade Readers Theatre: Picture Book Authors and Illustrators* by Suzanne I. Barchers and Charla R. Pfeffinger. Santa Barbara, CA: Teacher Ideas Press/Libraries Unlimited. Copyright © 2009.

May I Bring a Friend?

Beatrice Schenk de Regniers
1914–2001

Summary and Background Information

Born in Lafayette, Indiana, Beatrice Schenk de Regniers studied social work administration and later received a master's of education. She began writing for children in the 1950s, eventually combining a successful editorial role with writing. In this script, Mrs. Tully, the librarian, reads aloud the book *May I Bring a Friend?* by de Regniers. The book tells the story of a little boy who is invited to the palace for dinner. He asks if he may bring a friend. The first time he comes to dinner, he brings a giraffe. Each time he is invited to the palace, he asks the same question and brings different animals with him. Mrs. Tully uses the story as a model for discussion of special places that the children would like to go.

Presentation Suggestions

The narrators should sit on one side. The boys should be on one side and the girls on the other side of Mrs. Tully. There are specific lines for two boy and two girl readers. The remaining lines are in unison and can be read by any number of students. Before the readers say their questions or answers, they may pretend to be discussing their questions or answers. This should be a brief silent activity, mimed, and may need rehearsing.

Introductory and Follow-up Suggestions

If possible, read aloud *May I Bring a Friend?* Then ask:

- Who goes with you when you visit special places?
- What are your favorite special places?

27

After reading the book, ask:

- The author, Beatrice Schenk de Regniers, uses a repetitive pattern. What other stories use a pattern?

- What questions do you ask every day? (What time is it? What's for dinner? Can I turn on television? May I have a cookie?)

- What questions do your parents ask every day? (Do you have any homework? What did you do in school today?)

- How could you turn these questions into a repetitive pattern for a story?

Try doing a group story with one of the patterns. If time, have students write their own individual stories.

Characters

Grade One: Boy One, Girl One, Boy Two, Girl Two

Grade Two: Mrs. Tully, Girls, Boys

Grade Three: Narrator One, Narrator Two

May I Bring a Friend?

Narrator One: A group of children are at the library for story time. Today's story is *May I Bring a Friend?* The story is about a little boy. He is invited to dinner at the palace. When he is asked to dinner, he asks if he may bring a friend.

Narrator Two: When he goes to the palace, he takes an animal or two. The animals surprise the king and queen. They all have a very good time at the palace. Mrs. Tully asks the children where they would like to go that is special.

Mrs. Tully: In our story, the little boy went to the palace. We don't have palaces in the United States, do we? Where is a special place you would like to go?

Boy One: I would like to go to a water park.

Girl One: I would like to go to Disney World.

Boy Two: I would like to go to a theme park.

Girl Two: I would like to go eat pizza and play games.

Mrs. Tully: Let's play a word game. Pretend you are the little boy in the story. What would you ask me if I said, "Let's go to the water park."

Everyone: May I bring a friend?

Mrs. Tully: Yes, you may. Boys, I want you to ask the girls who they are going to bring. You need to tell them what the person is going to do. Their answer needs to rhyme with your question. Here is an example: Let's say the boys asked, "Who are you going to bring to swim with my mother?" What could you girls answer?

Girls: We are going to bring our older brother.

Mrs. Tully: Very good. All right boys, what is your first question?

Boys: Who are you going to bring to go down the giant twisting slide?

From *Multi-Grade Readers Theatre: Picture Book Authors and Illustrators* by Suzanne I. Barchers and Charla R. Pfeffinger. Santa Barbara, CA: Teacher Ideas Press/Libraries Unlimited. Copyright © 2009.

Girls: We are going to bring a beautiful bride.

Boys: Who are you going to bring to float on a rubber raft?

Girls: We are going to bring a brown and yellow giraffe.

Boys: Who are you going to bring to sunbathe on our towel?

Girls: We are going to bring a big horned owl.

Boys: Who are you going to bring to swim in the water?

Girls: We are going to bring a very fast otter.

Mrs. Tully: Very good. Let's change the place where we are going to go. Girls, you ask the questions this time. The boys will tell you who they are going bring. Now let's go to a theme park.

Everyone: May I bring a friend?

Mrs. Tully: Yes, you may.

Girls: Who are you going to bring to go down the water in a big, brown log?

Boys: We are going to bring a fat, green frog.

Girls: Who are you going to bring to ride on the huge twister?

Boys: We are going to bring our very brave sister.

Girls: Who are you going to bring to ride on the merry-go-round?

Boys: We are going to bring our dog that's a hound.

Girls: Who are you going to bring to ride on the twirling swings?

Boys: We are going to bring seven royal kings.

Girls: Who are you going to bring to ride on the park's train?

Boys: We are going to bring a whooping crane.

Mrs. Tully: This is so much fun! Let's change the place we are going to again. Girls, you will still ask the questions. Boys I want you to keep giving your clever answers. Now let's all go to Disney World!

Everyone: May I bring a friend?

From *Multi-Grade Readers Theatre: Picture Book Authors and Illustrators* by Suzanne I. Barchers and Charla R. Pfeffinger. Santa Barbara, CA: Teacher Ideas Press/Libraries Unlimited. Copyright © 2009.

Mrs. Tully: Yes, you may.

Girls: Who are you going to bring to ride in the Mad Hatter's teacup?

Boys: We are going to bring a cocker pup.

Girls: Who are you going to bring to do rides that spin?

Boys: We are going to bring all of our kin.

Girls: Who are you going to bring to ride on Donald Duck's boat?

Boys: We are going to bring a pigmy goat.

Girls: Who are you going to bring to ride along with Pooh?

Boys: We are going to bring Paul Bunyan and his ox, Babe the Blue.

Girls: Who are you going to bring to watch the big parade?

Boys: We are going to bring Zeke's cat named Jade.

Girls: Who are you going to bring to watch the fireworks?

Boys: We are going to bring two store clerks.

Mrs. Tully: Let's change the place we are going to go to again. Phyllis said she wanted to eat pizza and play games. This time, boys, you ask the questions and the girls will answer. Now let's go eat some pizza and play some games!

Everyone: May I bring a friend?

Mrs. Tully: Yes, you may.

Boys: Who are you going to bring to play air hockey?

Girls: We are going to bring Terri's cousin Rocky.

Boys: Who are you going to bring to challenge you at skee-ball?

Girls: We are going to bring Phyllis's Uncle Paul.

Boys: Who are you going to bring to race in the car?

Girls: We are going to bring Gerda's Aunt Starr.

Boys: Who are you going to bring to play pinball?

From *Multi-Grade Readers Theatre: Picture Book Authors and Illustrators* by Suzanne I. Barchers and Charla R. Pfeffinger. Santa Barbara, CA: Teacher Ideas Press/Libraries Unlimited. Copyright © 2009.

Girls: We are going to bring Angelee's brother Saul.

Mrs. Tully: We are out of time. I have one last question for all of you. What will you ask the next time your parents say your family is coming to the library?

Everyone: May I bring a friend?

Making Poetry

Aileen Fisher
1906–2002

Summary and Background Information

Aileen Lucia Fisher, an award-winning author of more than one hundred children's books, was born in Iron River, a small mining town in the Upper Peninsula of Michigan. She earned a degree in journalism and wrote stories, plays, poetry, biographies, and multimedia programs. Children who love poetry are most familiar with her many collections of poetry. Aileen Fisher lived in Boulder, Colorado for many years, inspired by the beauty of the mountains. This script explores a process for writing poetry. The readers will construct a poem using prompts from the teacher.

Presentation Suggestions

The narrator should be to the far side of the staging area. Mrs. White and Mr. Bakewell and the narrator should stand to one side, with the students on the other side. Their positions should allow them to read without their backs to the audience. If available, use a freestanding chart with paper or a chalkboard. During the reading, the reader for Mrs. White should write the lines of the poem on the chart paper or board as it develops. The script opens with Mrs. White sharing a poem by Aileen Fisher. A poem can be selected from one of these collections: *Heard a Bluebird Sing*, *Sing of the Earth and Sky: Poems about Our Planets and the Wonders Beyond*, *Cricket in a Thicket*, or *Feathered Ones and Furry*.

Introductory and Follow-up Suggestions

Share poetry from several favorite writers, including Aileen Fisher's. Then ask:

- What is a poem? How is it different from a short story or a novel?

- Have you ever tried to write a poem? What is hard about it? What is easy?

After reading the script, have the students write a poem individually or in small groups, using the process in this script as a model.

Characters

Grade One: Juanita, Norman, Peter, Millie

Grade Two: Kyle, Sabrina, Peggy, Maxine, Angelo, Mario

Grade Three: Narrator, Mrs. White, Mr. Bakewell

Making Poetry

Narrator: Today Mrs. White is going to help her class write a poem. One of the greatest poetry writers is Aileen Fisher. Mr. Bakewell knew Ms. Fisher before she died. He is going to help Mrs. White today. Ms. Fisher's poems are about the things you see or do every day. Mrs. White reads aloud one of Ms. Fisher's poems.

Mrs. White: *(Reads selected poem.)*

Juanita: That was a great poem! I wish I could write poetry.

Mrs. White: Would you like to learn how to write poetry like Ms. Fisher?

Everyone: Yes!

Norman: Is it easy to do?

Mrs. White: I don't think it is easy, but if you work real hard, you can do it.

Kyle: How do you get started when writing a poem?

Mr. Bakewell: Ms. Fisher said her ideas came to her from the things she did or read about. Some ideas came from things she remembered from growing up.

Sabrina: Once she got an idea, what did she do first?

Mr. Bakewell: She would write her first draft by hand with a pencil or a pen. Most writers start with a draft, which is a rough version of what they have in mind.

Peggy: What would Ms. Fisher do if she didn't like her first draft of a poem?

Mr. Bakewell: She would keep the things she liked and erase what she didn't like. Then she would re-read what she had left and add new thoughts. She would do this over and over again until she had her poem just the way she wanted it.

Sabrina: How long did it take her to write a poem?

From *Multi-Grade Readers Theatre: Picture Book Authors and Illustrators* by Suzanne I. Barchers and Charla R. Pfeffinger. Santa Barbara, CA: Teacher Ideas Press/Libraries Unlimited. Copyright © 2009.

Mr. Bakewell: I don't know for sure. I do know that she worked on her ideas for four hours every morning.

Juanita: What did she like to write about most?

Mr. Bakewell: She liked to write about animals and nature. She wrote about things she did.

Norman: Why did she write poetry?

Mr. Bakewell: She liked the rhythm, or the beat, of poetry. The words had to rhyme and make sense from line to line. Rhythm and rhyme make a poem fun to read.

Maxine: Can we write a poem together?

Mrs. White: All right. First someone has to decide what the poem is going to be about. Remember it should be a poem about something we all know.

Kyle: Everyone likes dogs or cats. How about cats?

Mrs. White: Now that we have a topic, we've started our poem. I'll write down "Cat" while you tell me what you already know about cats.

Sabrina: They get can be very fast when they are chasing a mouse.

Angelo: They love to play and really love to play with catnip.

Peggy: They love sitting in the sun and to clean their faces with their paws.

Peter: They can be big or small. Their fur can be different colors.

Mrs. White: Now that we have several good ideas, what should we do next?

Norman: We need to find some rhyming words.

Peter: We can change mouse to rat. Cat and rat rhyme.

Sabrina: If a cat eats too many rats he gets fat. That's another rhyming word.

Mrs. White: So let's put our ideas together to get our first line.

Angelo: I have two lines to start our poem. Once there was a cat. He napped upon a mat.

From *Multi-Grade Readers Theatre: Picture Book Authors and Illustrators* by Suzanne I. Barchers and Charla R. Pfeffinger. Santa Barbara, CA: Teacher Ideas Press/Libraries Unlimited. Copyright © 2009.

Millie: How about this next? That cat, he ate a rat.

Mario: When he is done eating the rat, he is really fat.

Mrs. White: How could you shorten that to continue the poem, Mario? So far we have "Once there was a cat. He napped upon a mat. That cat, he ate a rat."

Mario: What if we said, "He got so very fat"?

Millie: I like that, Mario. Can we read it aloud and see how it sounds?

Everyone: Once there was a cat. He napped upon a mat. That cat, he ate a rat. He got so very fat.

Norman: This is fun! Can we write some more lines, Mrs. White?

Mrs. White: Of course we can. Who has a line for another part of the poem?

Peggy: Well, he's pretty fat by now. So we could say something about how he weighed a ton.

Mrs. White: It would be an exaggeration, but that's fun in poetry. What words rhyme with ton?

Peter: Run, fun, bun, done.

Mrs. White: Which of those words can someone use in our poem?

Millie: We could say, "When his lunch was done, he must have weighed a ton."

Mrs. White: Very good. Now, if we could come up with a surprise ending, that would be especially fun.

Juanita: What if we told rats to stay away?

Mrs. White: That's very clever, Juanita. Can anyone think of a way to use that idea for the last two lines?

Maxine: We could say, "Our advice for a rat? Stay away from that cat!"

Kyle: Look, we have a real poem up there, Mrs. White!

Mrs. White: Yes we do. Let's read it now that it is finished.

From *Multi-Grade Readers Theatre: Picture Book Authors and Illustrators* by Suzanne I. Barchers and Charla R. Pfeffinger. Santa Barbara, CA: Teacher Ideas Press/Libraries Unlimited. Copyright © 2009.

Everybody: Once there was a cat. He napped upon a mat.
That cat, he ate a rat. He got so very fat.
When his lunch was done, he must have weighed a ton.
Our advice for a rat?
Stay away from that cat!

Mr. Bakewell: You all did a terrific job, and you made it look pretty easy, too. I have to leave now, but you have one more thing to do—decide on a title. Maybe the audience can help you! Goodbye!

Narrator: *(to the audience)* Can you help think up a clever title? After that, you might be ready to try writing some poetry of your own.

From *Multi-Grade Readers Theatre: Picture Book Authors and Illustrators* by Suzanne I. Barchers and Charla R. Pfeffinger. Santa Barbara, CA: Teacher Ideas Press/Libraries Unlimited. Copyright © 2009.

From Trumpeter to Artist

Don Freeman
1908–1978

Summary and Background Information

In this script, Don Freeman's father gives him a trumpet before his early death. Don, raised by a guardian, eventually goes to art school where he earns money playing his trumpet until he leaves it behind on a subway. He marries, has a son, and begins selling his sketches. Upon the advice of a librarian, he submits his book to a publisher. The script concludes with a visit to his son's art class.

Presentation Suggestions

The Freemans should stand in the middle. Father, the doctor, the art teacher, the librarian, and the narrators should stand on one side of the Freemans. Mr. Manley, Juanita, Ethan, Leigh, Jonathan, and Lila should stand on the other side.

Introductory and Follow-up Suggestions

Show the students a sketch pad. Then ask:

- What is this used for?

- How would it be useful if you were an art student?

After reading the script, discuss how Don and Lydia Freeman used their life experiences as part of the stories they created. Then ask:

- What other kinds of life experiences might contribute to stories that a writer tells?

- Artists keep sketches in a sketch pad. Where could writers keep notes, ideas, or short stories?

- What kinds of stories have you thought about writing or illustrating?

Characters

Grade One: Doctor, Lydia Freeman

Grade Two: Narrators One and Two, Don Freeman, Father, Librarian, Juanita, Ethan, Leigh, Jonathan

Grade Three: Art Teacher, Mr. Manley, Lila

From Trumpeter to Artist

Narrator One: Don Freeman, a young boy, gets a surprise from his father one day.

Father: Don, look what I have for you!

Don Freeman: Wow! Is that a musical instrument? What kind is it?

Father: It's a trumpet. You love music so much. I thought it was time you started learning to play an instrument.

Don Freeman: Thanks, Dad! Is it hard to play?

Father: It's hard to get started. But if you practice, you'll be good at it in no time. Look how good you have gotten by practicing with your drawing. I bet you'll be illustrating books in no time!

Narrator Two: Don works hard at playing the trumpet and at drawing. Then one day he gets terrible news from the doctor.

Doctor: I'm sorry to tell you this, Don. Your father has died.

Don Freeman: What is going to happen to me now?

Doctor: You'll be taken care of. Don't worry, son.

Narrator One: Don is raised by a guardian. He practices his drawing and his trumpet. He plays in a dance band. When he is a young adult, he decides to leave California and go to New York City. He goes to art school and works hard.

Art Teacher: Don, your drawings are improving, but I'm worried about you. How are you getting along? What are you doing for income? How do you pay for the models in your drawings?

Don Freeman: I'm doing okay. I study during the day and play my trumpet at night. I'm earning just enough money to get by. I'm sketching people on the subway. They don't seem to notice me.

Narrator Two: A few days later, Don looks very tired and sad.

From *Multi-Grade Readers Theatre: Picture Book Authors and Illustrators* by Suzanne I. Barchers and Charla R. Pfeffinger. Santa Barbara, CA: Teacher Ideas Press/Libraries Unlimited. Copyright © 2009.

Art Teacher: Don, you don't seem to be yourself today. Has something happened?

Don Freeman: I was sketching people on the subway last night. When I got off, I forgot my trumpet. I just stood there on the platform and watched it ride away.

Art Teacher: I'm so sorry, Don. What are you going to do?

Don Freeman: I'm going to try selling my work. I figure I'll start by doing sketches of people backstage during Broadway shows. Then I'll see if I can sell them to the newspapers and magazines.

Narrator One: Don succeeds with his sketches. Later, he marries Lydia, a woman he had met in an art class. They start a family and have a son named Roy. They live in an apartment near a set of railroad tracks. The sound of the trains being switched in the roundhouse each night often wakes them up.

Lydia Freeman: I am so tired of those trains waking us up at night.

Don Freeman: Me too. I've decided to do something about it. I'm going to go over there and draw the trains. Look at that caboose over there—it looks so lonely.

Lydia Freeman: You should do a book about it. You know, when I take Roy for a walk in the stroller, we pass the switchman. He has a small shack, and he even has a garden. Maybe he could be in the book.

Don Freeman: That's a great idea. Why don't I get some sketches done and then we can work on the plot together?

Narrator Two: Don and Lydia call the book *Chuggy and the Blue Caboose.* They take it to a librarian to see if she thinks children will like it.

Librarian: I really enjoyed your book, and I think children will love it. I think you should try to get it published.

Don Freeman: Where should we send it?

Librarian: There's a children's book editor at Viking Publishing. Why don't you send it there? She might like it, too.

Narrator One: *Chuggy and the Blue Caboose* is published and sells well. Many years later, Don and Lydia visit Roy's art class. They tell the story of how their first book started. The class is taught by Mr. Manley.

Mr. Manley: That's a wonderful story. We have been studying about how some picture books get published. I'd like some of the students to share what they have learned, and I know that they will have some questions. Would you start, Juanita?

Juanita: We looked at a lot of picture books. We were supposed to just look at the pictures and not read the stories.

Ethan: All the people who drew the pictures used a lot of colors. They all did different kinds of people, too.

Mr. Manley: What do you mean by different kinds of people, Ethan?

Ethan: Their shapes were all different—they had their own style. And you could tell who drew the pictures in a book by their style.

Lila: We also learned that some pictures were not drawn by the writer. They were added later by an artist.

Leigh: We also learned that some people can do both. They write and illustrate their books. They also might start with a folktale or a fable.

Juanita: How can it be that no one ever owned the story?

Mr. Manley: Many of the stories were just told. They weren't written down. No one really knows who first told the story. Also, there are many versions around.

Jonathan: I have a question. What is your favorite book, Mr. Freeman?

Don Freeman: That's easy. It's *Corduroy*. He was an orphan, like me. My father died when I was very young, and so *Corduroy* has a little bit of me in the story.

Lila: Did you always want to write and illustrate books?

From *Multi-Grade Readers Theatre: Picture Book Authors and Illustrators* by Suzanne I. Barchers and Charla R. Pfeffinger. Santa Barbara, CA: Teacher Ideas Press/Libraries Unlimited. Copyright © 2009.

Don Freeman: When I was a child, I never knew I would do books. I loved to draw, but it was the trumpet that led me to writing books.

Mr. Manley: Now, *that* sounds like a good story!

Don Freeman: You know, I think it is. Let me tell you the story. Once upon a time a father brought a young boy a trumpet . . . .

Narrator Two: And so the students learned a fine lesson—one good story leads to another.

From *Multi-Grade Readers Theatre: Picture Book Authors and Illustrators* by Suzanne I. Barchers and Charla R. Pfeffinger. Santa Barbara, CA: Teacher Ideas Press/Libraries Unlimited. Copyright © 2009.

Great Awards for Great Books

Ezra Jack Keats

1916–1983

Summary and Background Information

Ezra Jack Keats, distinguished for writing some of the earliest books featuring African American children, was born to a poor family in Brooklyn, New York. He showed his artistic talents as a young child, winning his first medal when he graduated from junior high school. Although times were difficult, his parents encouraged him to paint as much as they could afford. He worked during the day and took art classes at night. He worked as a mural painter and as a comic book illustrator before serving in the military during World War II. He built a career creating illustrations for various publications before becoming a children's book writer. This script discusses the role of awards conferred on his books and those of other outstanding illustrators and writers.

Presentation Suggestions

Gather a variety of award-winning books, including *The Snowy Day* by Ezra Jack Keats. Display them on a table. Include books that display medals on the covers. See www.ala.org for award possibilities, including awards such as the Caldecott Medal, Newbery Medal, Belpré Medal, Geisel Medal, and Wilder Award. See www.ezra-jack-keats.org for information about the Ezra Jack Keats Book Award. For the reading of the script, Mrs. Taylor and Mr. Wright should sit at one end by a table displaying the books. All other readers can be facing the audience in a semicircle.

Introductory and Follow-up Suggestions

Hold up several of the books that have won the Caldecott Medal. Then ask:

- What do you notice about the cover of these books? (Caldecott Medal)

- What do you know about this award?

- Have you ever won an award? If so, for what?

After reading the script, ask:

- Can you name other authors or illustrators who have won an award?

If the classroom has a computer for children to use, they can research the award lists at www.ala.org or www.ezra-jack-keats.org.

Characters

Grade One: Ernie, Maria, Patsy

Grade Two: Mrs. Taylor, Shelby, Samantha, Eddie, Trudy, Louie

Grade Three: Narrator, Mr. Wright, Pedro

Great Awards for Great Books

Narrator: Mr. Wright brings his students to the library. They are talking about books with Mrs. Taylor. She is the librarian.

Mrs. Taylor: Who has received an award for good grades?

Shelby and Ernie: I have.

Mrs. Taylor: What was your reward, Shelby?

Shelby: I got money for a good report card.

Ernie: So did I! I got one dollar for every A.

Mr. Wright: It shows that hard work pays off, doesn't it? Has anyone else gotten an award for something they have done?

Samantha: I did last year.

Mrs. Taylor: What was your award for, Samantha?

Samantha: My grandmother got sick and I went for help.

Mrs. Taylor: That was great, Samantha. What are some other things you could get an award for?

Eddie: I got a trophy for playing ball.

Pedro: Once I got a ribbon for running a race.

Maria: Oh, I got a ribbon once. I got it for my dog. He was the silliest dressed dog at the dog park.

Mr. Wright: Very good. Now we know that there are many different kinds of awards for things we do. Today, we are going to look at awards won by Ezra Jack Keats. Who knows who Ezra Jack Keats was?

Trudy: He was a writer. He wrote a lot of books.

Ernie: And he drew great pictures! I think they are the best part of his books.

Mrs. Taylor: Why do you say that, Ernie?

From *Multi-Grade Readers Theatre: Picture Book Authors and Illustrators* by Suzanne I. Barchers and Charla R. Pfeffinger. Santa Barbara, CA: Teacher Ideas Press/Libraries Unlimited. Copyright © 2009.

Ernie: He used such great colors in his pictures. My little brother loves to look at them.

Mrs. Taylor: Many of Keats's books won awards.

Eddie: Why would you give a book an award?

Mr. Wright: Does anyone know the answer to Eddie's question?

Pedro: Because the book tells a very good story.

Maria: And he did draw some great pictures.

Samantha: What was the award, Mrs. Taylor?

Mrs. Taylor: *The Snowy Day* won the Caldecott Medal for its drawings.

Patsy: How can you tell if a book won an award?

Mrs. Taylor: I looked on the back cover of *The Snowy Day*. The back cover tells about the award. On some books there are medals on the front cover.

Louie: Is that the only award *The Snowy Day* won?

Mr. Wright: No. It got the Brooklyn Art Books for Children Citation, also.

Shelby: Are there other awards out there for books?

Mrs. Taylor: Oh, yes. There are many of them. Here let me show you some other books with awards on them. (*Show a variety of award-winning books.*)

Eddie: Do you know what book has won the most awards ever?

Mrs. Taylor: No, I don't Eddie. I do know there are a lot of books in our library that have each won one or more awards.

Pedro: Did Keats win an award for any other book?

Mrs. Taylor: Yes. *Goggles* received the Caldecott Honor Book award. Later on, Mr. Keats decided to give awards to other writers for their hard work.

Samantha: You mean there is an Ezra Jack Keats Award? Why?

Mr. Wright: Mr. Keats wanted to encourage other artists. He was very poor and couldn't afford to go to art school. So he worked all day and went to art school at night. He lived during the

Great Depression and World War II. Those were tough times. An award like this one lets other people know that the artist is special.

Ernie: Did he win any medals when he was going to school?

Mr. Wright: He won his very first medal in junior high. He kept it all his life with his other awards.

Patsy: Did he do other kinds of art?

Mr. Wright: He did murals and drawings for magazines. He even did drawings for comic books! It took him a while to get a children's book published.

Maria: I think we should start a reading club. We should read only books that have won an award.

Trudy: That's a great idea, Maria. Can we do that, Mrs. Taylor?

Mrs. Taylor: I think it's a great idea, too. If you would like to start a reading club, I'll be happy to help you.

Pedro: How will we know what books have won awards? There are so many books in here!

Mrs. Taylor: I can give you book lists. Then you can go down the list and choose the books you want to read.

Maria: We need a goal for our reading club.

Samantha: What would be our goal?

Louie: We should have to read three award-winning books a week. Then we could talk about them.

Ernie: Would reading to my brother count?

Mrs. Taylor: That is a very good idea, Ernie. Yes, that would count.

Eddie: Why would you want to read to your brother, Ernie?

Ernie: He loves the pictures in Keats's books. And he likes to hear those stories.

Patsy: And they are easy to read, right Mrs. Taylor?

From *Multi-Grade Readers Theatre: Picture Book Authors and Illustrators* by Suzanne I. Barchers and Charla R. Pfeffinger. Westport, CT: Teacher Ideas Press/Libraries Unlimited. Copyright © 2009.

Mrs. Taylor: Even if they are easy to read, it is still reading. Some of you will want to read easier books, and that is okay. The important thing is you are reading. I am excited about your clubs. I'll have a list of books for you to read tomorrow. See you then.

Mr. Wright: Time to get back to class, children. See you tomorrow, Mrs. Taylor.

Who's a Fat Cat?

John Wellington (Jack) Kent
1920–1985

Summary and Background Information

Jack Kent was born in Burlington, Iowa. He began his career as a freelance commercial artist at the age of fifteen. He worked until he joined the U.S. Army, Field Artillery, in 1941. His syndicated comic strip, "King Aroo," was distributed internationally from 1950 to 1965. When it was dropped from the newspapers, he returned to working as a cartoonist and humorist. Another short-lived strip was "Why Christmas Almost Wasn't." in 1968. His retelling of old classics using his unique illustrations produced wonderful children's books that are still read today. He died of leukemia in 1985. This script is based on the Danish tale *The Fat Cat*. The following are a few of the well-known books by Kent: *The Bremen Town Musicians*, *Seven at One Blow,* a non-violent collection of rhymes for the young in *Merry Mother Goose,* and two books based on *Fables of Aesop.*

Presentation Suggestions

The narrators and Mrs. Herrera can sit to one side of the staging area. The reader for Mr. Snyder should sit facing the narrators on the opposite side of the staging area. The other readers can sit in the center slightly facing Mr. Snyder.

Introductory and Follow-up Suggestions

Read aloud *The Fat Cat* by Jack Kent. Then ask:

- What does an illustrator do?

- Why are pictures important in a book?

- Can you tell who a book's illustrator is by looking at his pictures? How?

- What is the most important thing about an illustration to you?

After reading the script, find a collection of Aesop's fables without illustrations. Copy a fable and have the children read and illustrate it.

Characters

Grade One: Josie, Jerald

Grade Two: Narrator Two, Marrie, Mr. Snyder, Levi, Della, Wilson, Mrs. Herrera, Mr. Petersen

Grade Three: Narrator One, Latashia

Who's a Fat Cat?

Narrator One: Many children live in the high-rise on Spring Street. They live far from the library. Each Saturday morning, a library comes to them. Mr. Snyder is the librarian. He drives and runs this library on wheels.

Narrator Two: On nice days, Mr. Snyder has story time outside. He pulls out the awning on the side of the bus. He puts out his chair and a small table. On the table is the book he is going to read to the children. The children are always happy to see him arrive.

Marrie: Hurry up, Josie. Mr. Snyder's going to read a story today.

Josie: I am hurrying up.

Marrie: Do you have your books to turn in?

Josie: Yes, and I have my mat. I'm ready. Let's go!

Narrator One: The children gather under the awning, ready for story time. Mr. Snyder comes out of the bus. This time the table is empty. Instead, he holds a book behind his back.

Mr. Snyder: Good morning. Are you ready to hear a story today?

Everyone: Yes. What are you going to read?

Mr. Snyder: I am going to read one of our favorites. It is about a cat. Let's see if you can guess which book it is. (Mr. Snyder blows his cheeks up real fat.)

Everyone: *The Fat Cat*!

Mr. Snyder: Yes, I am going to read *The Fat Cat*. But first I want to ask you some questions. Who remembers who wrote the book *The Fat Cat*?

Jerald: The book was written by Jack Kent. But it wasn't his story.

Mr. Snyder: Good memory, Jerald. Since it wasn't his story, where did it come from?

From *Multi-Grade Readers Theatre: Picture Book Authors and Illustrators* by Suzanne I. Barchers and Charla R. Pfeffinger. Santa Barbara, CA: Teacher Ideas Press/Libraries Unlimited. Copyright © 2009.

Levi: First it was a Danish folktale. Mr. Kent retold the tale in his book. And he drew cartoon-like pictures for the book.

Mr. Snyder: Why is the book called *The Fat Cat?*

Latashia: It's about a greedy cat. It eats anything it sees and gets really fat.

Mr. Snyder: Are you ready for me to read the book?

Everyone: Yes.

Narrator Two: Mr. Snyder reads *The Fat Cat* to the children. The people in the high-rise can hear the children laugh as he reads the book. Some of the parents come down to see what is so funny.

Narrator One: When Mr. Snyder looks up he sees a lot of parents listening to the story. He is surprised to see them. Even the parents laugh as the cat gets fat. Finally, he finishes the story.

Mr. Snyder: That is such a funny story. Are any of you fat cats?

Della: No! I think every one of us is smarter than that cat. If any of us ate thirty-five pies, we'd get sick before we got fat!

Wilson: And I don't know anyone who would eat a real person.

Della: And I sure wouldn't eat an elephant!

Josie: I am glad I am not greedy like that fat cat.

Marrie: I am glad our mama taught us good manners. I would hate it if you did "slip slop, sluuurp" when you ate.

Everyone: Slip slop, sluuurp, slip slop, sluuurp!

Mr. Snyder: (laughs) I am glad to know none of you is a fat cat. Does anyone have any questions before we check out books?

Mrs. Herrera: I would like to know who wrote the book you just read to the children.

Everyone: Jack Kent. He drew the pictures, too.

Mrs. Herrera: Oh, my. You *all* knew that! Mr. Snyder, do you always tell them about the writers?

From *Multi-Grade Readers Theatre: Picture Book Authors and Illustrators* by Suzanne I. Barchers and Charla R. Pfeffinger. Santa Barbara, CA: Teacher Ideas Press/Libraries Unlimited. Copyright © 2009.

Mr. Snyder: Yes, I do. A book is a reflection of someone. They need to know about the person who writes and illustrates the book.

Mr. Petersen: What can any of you tell me about Jack Kent?

Levi: He created a comic strip. It was called . . .

Everyone: King Aroo.

Latashia: He drew postcards for a card company.

Della: He drew pictures for a lot of books. He also did funny fables.

Jerald: He drew pictures to go with rhymes and folktales, too.

Wilson: He didn't write any books with his own words. He retold good stories and drew the pictures.

Mr. Petersen: You all sure do know a lot about Jack Kent. I would like to read some of his books to my children. Can I check out *The Fat Cat*, Mr. Snyder?

Mr. Snyder: Of course you can. I have several of his books inside you might want also. Is everyone ready to check out new books?

Narrator One: Books were different years ago. They had many short stories in them but no pictures.

Narrator Two: The pictures make this book more fun. The fat cat wouldn't be as funny if you couldn't see him get fatter and fatter.

Narrator One: A good illustrator can take an old story and make it seem like new. Pictures can make us laugh, cry, or think about the plot. They can even help us read the words. We can see what is happening through the pictures.

Narrator Two: Have you ever tried to draw pictures from words you have read? Why not try it? Maybe you can be an illustrator one day.

From *Multi-Grade Readers Theatre: Picture Book Authors and Illustrators* by Suzanne I. Barchers and Charla R. Pfeffinger. Santa Barbara, CA: Teacher Ideas Press/Libraries Unlimited. Copyright © 2009.

The Trouble with a Pen Name

James Edward Marshall
1942–1992

Summary and Background Information

James Edward Marshall diligently studied the viola as a way to move away from Texas. He won a scholarship to the New England Conservatory in Boston. Unfortunately, a hand injury cut short his musical career. Marshall had always had an interest in drawing, but he had given up the practice in the second grade when a teacher had laughed at his artwork. He picked up the hobby once again and a friend saw his sketches and brought them to a neighbor who worked at Houghton Mifflin. When an editor there saw the drawing, he offered Marshall a contract for his first assignment. This first book, Byrd Baylor's *Plink, Plink, Plink*, was published in 1971. This opened up a new career path for Marshall, whose legacy lives on in more than seventy books that he has written or illustrated.

Presentation Suggestions

The narrator and Mrs. White should sit on either side of the stage. James Marshall should sit facing the audience with the other characters in a semicircle around him.

Introductory and Follow-up Suggestions

Read aloud *George and Martha* and *Fox at School.* Show the covers. Then ask:

- What is alike and what is different about the books?
- What other books did James Marshall write? Edward Marshall?

After reading the script, discuss other reasons why people might use a pen name. Ask:

- What is another word for a pen name? (pseudonym)
- What was Mark Twain's real name? (Samuel Clemens)
- What are other reasons why a person might use a pen name?
- If you were going to use a pen name, what would it be?

Characters

Grade One: Gavin, Billie, Riley, Mrs. White

Grade Two: Irene, Henry, Walt, Opal, Marguerite

Grade Three: Narrator, James Marshall, Cecilia, Russ

The Trouble with a Pen Name

Narrator: Mrs. White has asked James Marshall to talk with her class. They are going to write an article about him for the school newspaper. Gavin asks the first question.

Gavin: How do you get your ideas?

James Marshall: My ideas come from my daydreams and doodles. Once I have a character drawn, then I write my story.

Irene: Do you always work alone?

James Marshall: No. I often work with another author.

Cecilia: What is your favorite thing to do with a story line?

James Marshall: I want to make readers laugh. Reading should be fun. If my stories make you laugh, you will read more.

Henry: What is the title of the first book you ever wrote?

James Marshall: My first book was *George and Martha.* One day I saw two dots on my drawing paper. I added two more dots, and behold! I had the eyes of George and Martha. I loved doing George and Martha because I could make them funny. It didn't matter what happened to them. They were always best friends.

Walt: Are they the characters you like the most?

James Marshall: I like them a lot because they were in my first book. But Viola Swamp has to be the one I like most of all. Do you know who she is?

Opal: That awful teacher in the book *Miss Nelson Is Missing.*

James Marshall: Yes, she is. And can you guess where I got the idea for her?

Billie: Was she one of your teachers?

James Marshall: She looks just like my second-grade teacher who laughed at me.

From *Multi-Grade Readers Theatre: Picture Book Authors and Illustrators* by Suzanne I. Barchers and Charla R. Pfeffinger. Santa Barbara, CA: Teacher Ideas Press/Libraries Unlimited. Copyright © 2009.

Russ: Did your teacher ever see herself in your book?

James Marshall: Yes, she saw the book. She told me she thought it was amusing that I used her as the wicked teacher. So I don't feel too terrible about using her as my model.

Gavin: Did you always want to write and draw for books?

James Marshall: No. When I was a young boy I wanted to play the viola. I was very good. I won a scholarship to go to the New England Conservatory in Boston. Then one day I was in a plane and I injured my hand. I could only play my viola for a few minutes a day. I had to give up that dream.

Cecilia: What did you do after your accident?

James Marshall: I went to college. I got a degree to teach. Then I started doodling as a hobby. A friend gave my doodlings to someone who worked in a publishing house. They asked me to do drawings for a book.

Billie: What was the book called?

James Marshall: *Plink, Plink, Plink.*

Irene: Was it a great success like your other books?

James Marshall: No, it flopped. But that is when I knew I wanted to become an illustrator and writer.

Russ: Who did you co-author the Miss Nelson books with?

James Marshall: Harry Allard. We did two different series. The first was the Miss Nelson Books. Then we did the Stupid Family Books. Have you read any of the Stupid Family Books? Did they make you laugh?

Opal: I laughed so hard at them, I cried. Do you think people are really that stupid?

James Marshall: I hope not. To think you are dead just because the lights go out is really stupid. But if it made you laugh, then it was what we wanted you to do.

Henry: I thought they were very funny. But I am sure glad I am not that stupid.

James Marshall: I think we all feel stupid sometimes. But no one is as stupid as the Stupids are. When you read about how stupid they are, you don't feel so stupid yourself.

Walt: What other series of books did you write?

James Marshall: I wrote a series of books about a fox. I didn't want anyone to know I was writing it. I used a pen name. I pretended my cousin, Edward Marshall, wrote the books.

Riley: Why would you do that?

James Marshall: I had a contract with a publishing house. It said I had to do all my books with them. I had these great stories in my head. They were to be stories that were easy-to-read books. I couldn't publish them under my contract. If I changed my name, then I could get them published. Now some people write under different names because people expect certain things in their books.

Opal: Oh, I bet I know what you mean. In all of your books you drew certain things in the pictures. Like the fat cat was in a lot of your books.

James Marshall: Very good. That is exactly the kind of things I mean. Readers expect to see certain things. Does anyone remember anything else that I often put in my pictures?

Marguerite: There were stacks of things in the pictures. Some of them would be about to fall over.

James Marshall: You are a very alert group of readers!

Mrs. White: Yes, they are. Our time is almost up, Mr. Marshall.

James Marshall: Do I have time to tell you what happened to me as Edward Marshall?

Mrs. White: I think so.

From *Multi-Grade Readers Theatre: Picture Book Authors and Illustrators* by Suzanne I. Barchers and Charla R. Pfeffinger. Westport, CT: Teacher Ideas Press/Libraries Unlimited. Copyright © 2009.

James Marshall: There is moral to this story. When I used the name Edward Marshall, I told the editor he was my cousin. The editor didn't think I was writing the book. I said he lived in Texas. One day the editor called me. He said he couldn't get ahold of my cousin. He needed to ask him some questions about his background. He asked me if I could tell him some things about Edward.

Mrs. White: You got caught, didn't you?

James Marshall: Not right then. But I did have to tell him something. I made up this big story about my cousin. He believed it. They printed this story on the cover of the book! So what is the moral of the story?

Marguerite: Tell your editor if you want to use a pen name.

Riley: And always tell the truth!

James Marshall: I think that's pretty good advice.

Narrator: Mr. Marshall says goodbye. Then the students start writing their article for the school newspaper. They *don't* use a pen name!

From *Multi-Grade Readers Theatre: Picture Book Authors and Illustrators* by Suzanne I. Barchers and Charla R. Pfeffinger. Santa Barbara, CA: Teacher Ideas Press/Libraries Unlimited. Copyright © 2009.

What Do You See?

Bill Martin Jr.

1916–2004

Summary and Background Information

Bill Martin Jr. grew up in Kansas, in a family with limited resources. Although he loved stories and the sounds of the language, he didn't learn how to read until college. It took a college professor to convince him to read a book, cover to cover. He became a teacher, principal, and highly regarded author of more than three hundred books. The one that most aptly demonstrates his appreciation of language and his determination to give children books that they can read successfully is *Brown Bear, Brown Bear, What Do You See?*, illustrated by Eric Carle. This script, drawn from many interviews with Bill Martin Jr., provides an overview of key events in his life. The lines read by Speaker One through Speaker Twelve can be collapsed into fewer parts if necessary.

Presentation Suggestions

The narrators can stand together on one side. Speaker One through Speaker Twelve should stand with the responding reader. For example, Speaker One should stand with Grandmother, Speaker Two should stand with Mother, and so forth.

Introductory and Follow-up Suggestions

Read aloud *Brown Bear, Brown Bear, What Do You See?* Identify the author and illustrator of the book. Explain that the author, Bill Martin Jr., died in 2004. Then ask:

- What makes this book easy to read?

- Can you name any other books by Bill Martin Jr.?

- If you could ask Bill Martin Jr. any questions, what would you ask him?

After reading the script, ask:

- *Brown Bear, Brown Bear, What Do You See?* is called a pattern book because it follows a predictable pattern. What are the key parts to the pattern? (an adjective plus a noun that is repeated, followed by a question and an answer)

- What else could be used for a pattern? Think about people, places, things, numbers, sizes, adverbs, prepositional phrases, exclamatory sentences, and the like.

If time allows, create a group story that uses a pattern.

Characters

Grade One: Speaker One, Speaker Two, Speaker Three, Speaker Four, Father, Speaker Five, Professor, Speaker Nine, Speaker Twelve

Grade Two: Narrator Two, Grandmother, Speaker Six, Speaker Seven, Speaker Eight, Speaker Ten, Eric Carle

Grade Three: Mother, Mrs. Davis, Drama Teacher, Speaker Eleven

Grade Four: Narrator One, Bernard, Teacher, Publisher, Michael Sampson, Bill Martin Jr.

What Do You See?

Narrator One: Bill Martin Jr. died on August 11, 2004. He wrote more than three hundred books during his fifty years as a writer. Almost every child knows one of his books. It is *Brown Bear, Brown Bear, What Do You See?*

Narrator Two: Many people helped Bill along the way. Some have also died. Some are still alive. If each one could answer a question about Bill, this is what each might say.

Speaker One: Bill Martin's grandmother, what did you see? What did he like to do?

Grandmother: I saw a boy who loved to listen to stories. We worked hard in those days, but there was always time for a good story.

Speaker Two: Bill Martin's mother, what did you see? Can you tell us about his name?

Mother: I saw a boy who was named after his father and me. His father was named William. My name was Iva. We named him William Ivan. He got teased about the name Ivan. He left it out of his name, and people assumed he was William Martin Jr. That's how he became Bill Martin Jr.

Speaker Three: Bill Martin's fifth-grade teacher, what did you see? Was he a good student?

Mrs. Davis: I taught fifth grade. I read aloud to the students twice a day. Bill loved listening to the stories. He especially liked *Treasure Island.* He didn't read very well, but he was very good with language.

Speaker Four: Bill Martin's father, what did you see? Did he grow up to be like you?

Father: We didn't have any books in our home. But I loved animals, and Bill shared that love. You can see his love of animals in the books he's written.

From *Multi-Grade Readers Theatre: Picture Book Authors and Illustrators* by Suzanne I. Barchers and Charla R. Pfeffinger. Santa Barbara, CA: Teacher Ideas Press/Libraries Unlimited. Copyright © 2009.

Speaker Five: Bill Martin's high school teacher, what did you see? What did Bill like about high school?

Drama Teacher: I was Bill's drama teacher. He loved William Shakespeare's plays. He couldn't read them well, but he loved the sounds of the language.

Speaker Six: Bill Martin's professor, what did you see? How did Bill do in college?

Professor: Bill was in my writing class, and he still couldn't read well. One day I brought him some books to read. I told him that if he wanted to write, he needed to learn to read. Bill worked hard at it, and he taught himself how to read.

Speaker Seven: Bill Martin's brother, what did you see? What did Bill do after college?

Bernard: Bill taught English and drama after college. He went into the military during World War II. But the best memory I have is that we worked on his very first book together. I had been injured during the war. Bill had written a story called "The Little Squeegy Bug." He asked me to illustrate it. That kept me busy while I was getting better. We did eleven books together during the next ten years.

Speaker Eight: Bill Martin's teacher friend, what did you see? How did you know him?

Teacher: I knew Bill when he was a principal. He worked very hard at all that he did. He even got a doctorate in education! You always knew that reading aloud and the beauty of language were important to Bill.

Speaker Nine: Bill Martin's publisher friend, what did you see? What did Bill do with you?

Publisher: Bill developed a wonderful reading series. He used the same ideas he had used to learn to read. He relied on the sounds of language to engage readers. He also believed that kids should be able to read something on their first day of first grade. They should be able to say, "I did it!" That was so important to Bill.

From *Multi-Grade Readers Theatre: Picture Book Authors and Illustrators* by Suzanne I. Barchers and Charla R. Pfeffinger. Santa Barbara, CA: Teacher Ideas Press/Libraries Unlimited. Copyright © 2009.

Speaker Ten: Bill Martin's illustrator, what did you see? How did you and Bill meet?

Eric Carle: Bill found me. I had designed a red lobster for a magazine ad. Bill saw it and asked me to illustrate *Brown Bear, Brown Bear, What Do You See?* He had written that book on a train ride. Being asked to work with him changed my life. I started writing and illustrating my own books.

Speaker Eleven: Bill Martin's writing partner, what do you see? How did you get together?

Michael Sampson: We met in 1977 while I was getting my PhD in reading. We both loved children's books, and that started our friendship. My family and I lived near Bill for several years before he died. We would write together at his kitchen table.

Narrator Two: Bill Martin Jr. gave many interviews before he died. Let's let his words speak to us now.

Speaker Twelve: Bill Martin Jr., what do you see? What else can you tell us about your writing?

Bill Martin Jr.: If anyone had told me that I was going to be a writer of children's books when I was a child, I would have said, "You're badly mistaken. I can't even read." I still am a very slow reader, but I'm an avid reader. I read all the time. Students will only learn to read when they have language inside of themselves.

From *Multi-Grade Readers Theatre: Picture Book Authors and Illustrators* by Suzanne I. Barchers and Charla R. Pfeffinger. Santa Barbara, CA: Teacher Ideas Press/Libraries Unlimited. Copyright © 2009.

Make Way for McCloskey

Robert McCloskey

1914–2003

Summary and Background Information

Robert McCloskey took piano lessons as a child and planned to pursue music for his career. Then he discovered how much fun it was to invent things. In high school, he learned how much he loved art and drawing. In art school, he painted in oil, but no one bought his art. That led him to writing and illustrating for children. He was inspired to write *Make Way for Ducklings* after observing the ducks in Boston Garden when walking to art school. Mr. McCloskey won a Caldecott Medal for *Make Way for Ducklings* in 1942 and a Caldecott Medal for *Time of Wonder* in 1958. He won Caldecott Honor awards for *Blueberries for Sal, One Morning in Maine,* and *Journey Cake Ho!* In this script, Mr. Mallard, featured in *Make Way for Ducklings,* returns to his family and shares the exciting news that Robert McCloskey has won the Caldecott Medal. He also describes how Mr. McCloskey brought mallards into his studio in New York City to learn how to draw them.

Presentation Suggestions

The narrators can be on one side with Mr. and Mrs. Mallard on the other side. The ducklings can stand or sit in the middle. To accommodate more students, there can be more ducklings. Students reading the duck parts can wear extra large yellow T-shirts over their clothes and nametags with the ducks' names.

Introductory and Follow-up Suggestions

Show students where Boston and New York City are on a map. Then ask:

- Have you visited either Boston or New York City? What is it like?

- Do you think a big city is a good place for a family of ducks? Why or why not?

Read aloud *Make Way for Ducklings* and have students read the script. Then ask the following questions:

- In the script the ducks talk to each other. Do you think animals can communicate? Why or why not? Explain that sometimes writers give animals human abilities, which is called anthropomorphism. Discuss other books that use anthropomorphism.

- What did you learn from the script that isn't in the book?

Characters

Grade One: Jack, Kack, Lack, Mack, Nack, Oack, Pack, Quack

Grade Two: Mrs. Mallard, Mr. Mallard

Grade Three: Narrator One, Narrator Two

Make Way for McCloskey

Narrator One: Eight ducklings swim in a lagoon in Boston. They are named Jack, Kack, Lack, Mack, Nack, Ouack, Pack, and Quack. Mrs. Mallard watches while they swim.

Narrator Two: All of a sudden they hear wings flapping. Mr. Mallard flies down to the water. He paddles in big circles.

Mrs. Mallard: You look like you have exciting news for us. What has happened?

Mr. Mallard: I have very big news! It's about Mr. McCloskey.

Mrs. Mallard: What is it? Is he okay?

Mr. Mallard: Don't you worry about Mr. McCloskey, my dear. He told me the big news himself.

Jack, Kack, Lack, Mack: Tell us, Papa! Tell us the big news!

Mrs. Mallard: Yes, tell us what he said. We all want to know.

Nack, Oack, Pack, and Quack: Tell us now! We can't wait.

Mr. Mallard: Well, he won a big award.

Jack, Kack, Lack, Mack: What is an award?

Mr. Mallard: An award is like a big prize.

Nack, Oack, Pack, and Quack: Why did he get an award?

Mr. Mallard: This award is called the Caldecott Medal. He got it for the drawings in one of his books. Guess which book!

Mrs. Mallard: It must be for the book about us!

Mr. Mallard: That's right, dear. Do you remember the book, children?

Jack, Kack, Lack, Mack: Tell us the story! Tell us the story!

From *Multi-Grade Readers Theatre: Picture Book Authors and Illustrators* by Suzanne I. Barchers and Charla R. Pfeffinger. Santa Barbara, CA: Teacher Ideas Press/Libraries Unlimited. Copyright © 2009.

Quack: I know how it starts! I remember it all.

Mrs. Mallard: You can't remember some of the story. It starts a bit before you were born.

Narrator One: Mrs. Mallard talks to her children. She tells how she and Mr. Mallard looked for a safe place to raise a family. They started out at the Public Garden. But a boy on a bike almost ran her over.

Mrs. Mallard: We looked everywhere to make our nest. Then we found just the place, an island in the Charles River. That's where we met our good friend, Michael. He is a policeman. He would feed us lots of peanuts.

Quack: I remember him! I used to eat *all* the peanuts.

Nack, Oack, Pack: No you didn't!

Quack: Yes, I did!

Mr. Mallard: No, Quack, you still hadn't arrived. But that is the next part of our story! Eight ducklings hatched and we named you . . . .

All the Ducklings: Jack, Kack, Lack, Mack, Nack, Ouack, Pack, and Quack!

Mrs. Mallard: That's right! Your father decided to look for a good home again. So he left us for a week. I started giving you lessons on how to be good little ducklings. That week was so very busy. Soon it was time to meet your father in the Public Garden.

Quack: I know what happened next. I was there!

Mrs. Mallard: Yes, you were there, Quack. We had to get across some busy streets to get to the Public Garden. Those cars would just whiz by. No one would stop for us until Michael helped us. He stopped the traffic, and then he had his friends help us get to the Public Garden safely.

From *Multi-Grade Readers Theatre: Picture Book Authors and Illustrators* by Suzanne I. Barchers and Charla R. Pfeffinger. Santa Barbara, CA: Teacher Ideas Press/Libraries Unlimited. Copyright © 2009.

Mr. Mallard: And there I was, waiting for all of you! Your mother and I decided this was the best place to live. We have been here ever since that day.

All the Ducklings: Yeah!

Mr. Mallard: I found out some other things.

Mrs. Mallard: What did you find out? Are they about Mr. McCloskey or about the book?

Mr. Mallard: They are about both. Mr. McCloskey didn't make the book here in Boston. He used to come here to feed the ducks. Of course, that was before our time. But he wrote the story and made all the drawings somewhere else.

Mrs. Mallard: Where was he living?

Mr. Mallard: He lived in New York City.

All the Ducklings: New York City!

Mrs. Mallard: How did he make such good drawings? He must have looked at a lot of pictures of ducks. I don't think there are many ducks in New York City.

Mr. Mallard: There are ducks in a big park called Central Park. But he didn't go there. He bought some baby mallards and took them right to his studio!

Quack: What's a studio?

Mr. Mallard: It's a place where artists can draw or paint.

Mrs. Mallard: Wouldn't that be kind of . . . messy? What did Mr. McCloskey do about . . . well . . . about you know . . .

Mr. Mallard: He said he followed those ducklings everywhere. He even let them swim in his bathtub! He made lots of drawings of them. Then he'd use tissues to clean up after them!

From *Multi-Grade Readers Theatre: Picture Book Authors and Illustrators* by Suzanne I. Barchers and Charla R. Pfeffinger. Santa Barbara, CA: Teacher Ideas Press/Libraries Unlimited. Copyright © 2009.

Mrs. Mallard: I'm glad I don't have to clean up after all of you. I would be too busy to even take a swim!

Mr. Mallard: Children, I have a question for you. What is the name of Mr. McCloskey's book?

All the Ducklings: *Make Way for Ducklings!*

Quack: Do you think they'll make a movie next?

Mrs. Mallard: You never know, dear. You never know.

Narrator Two: Robert McCloskey didn't plan to be a writer and an artist. He planned to be a musician. He learned to play the piano, the drums, and the oboe when he was a young boy. He played one other instrument. You can find out what it was if you look at the cover of his book *Lentil.* Best of all—he grew up to make great books for children!

From *Multi-Grade Readers Theatre: Picture Book Authors and Illustrators* by Suzanne I. Barchers and Charla R. Pfeffinger. Santa Barbara, CA: Teacher Ideas Press/Libraries Unlimited. Copyright © 2009.

'Twas the Night before Christmas

Clement Clarke Moore

1779–1863

Summary and Background Information

Clement Clarke Moore is credited with writing *A Visit from St. Nicholas*, also known as *'Twas the Night before Christmas*. In 1855, one of his daughters, Mary C. Moore Ogden, painted "illuminations" to go with *A Visit from St. Nicholas,* which was later published as a book. Clement Clarke Moore was more famous in his own day as a professor of Asian and Greek literature at Columbia College, now Columbia University. He was also a professor of biblical learning at the General Theological Seminary in New York. While there, he compiled a two-volume Hebrew and English lexicon. He also published a collection of poems in 1844.

Presentation Suggestions

The readability for groups one and two is at grade one. Groups three and four have variations in the reading levels. The readers will have to pay close attention to the script, as they do not always read in chronological order. Select as many readers as you want for the groups. The narrator should sit on the far side of the staging area. The groups should sit or stand in the middle of the staging area. The children and Mrs. English should sit on the other side of the staging area.

Introductory and Follow-up Suggestions

Before reading the script, ask the following questions:

- What are some of your favorite Christmas stories or poems?

- Can you name the eight reindeer in *'Twas the Night before Christmas*?

- Who is the ninth reindeer pulling Santa's sled?

After reading the script, ask:

• Can you remember the names of all the reindeer?

Characters

Grade One: Group One, Group Two, Frank

Grade Two: Lisa, Mama, Mrs. English, Gabe, Brody, Stacey, Missy

Grade Three: Narrator, Group Three, Group Four

'Twas the Night before Christmas

Narrator: It is almost Christmas. Lisa has gotten some mail.

Lisa: Mama, look at what I got in the mail today.

Mama: What is it, Lisa?

Lisa: It says Mrs. English is going to have a party. You are invited to come, too. Will you go with me?

Mama: Of course I will go with you. I really love parties, especially at this time of year.

Narrator: It is the day of the big party. All the boys and girls and their parents have arrived.

Mrs. English: It is so nice so many of you could come today. To begin with, I need all the adults to join me in the break room. We'll be right back.

Gabe: I wonder why she wants to meet with our parents.

Brody: I bet they are planning a surprise.

Stacey: I can't wait to see what they are planning. Mrs. English is so clever! I know it'll be a lot of fun.

Frank: Here they come. What do they have in their hands?

Missy: It looks like they are carrying papers.

Mrs. English: I have asked the adults to read a poem to you.

Frank: Is it a Christmas poem?

Mrs. English: Yes, it is. Can anyone guess the name of the poem?

Everyone: *'Twas the Night before Christmas!*

Mrs. English: You are so smart! Let's listen to the adults read *'Twas the Night before Christmas!*

Group One: 'Twas the night before Christmas, when all through the house

Group Two: Not a creature was stirring, not even a mouse;

From *Multi-Grade Readers Theatre: Picture Book Authors and Illustrators* by Suzanne I. Barchers and Charla R. Pfeffinger. Santa Barbara, CA: Teacher Ideas Press/Libraries Unlimited. Copyright © 2009.

Group One: The stockings were hung by the chimney with care,

Group Two: In hopes that St. Nicholas soon would be there;

Group One: The children were nestled all snug in their beds,

Group Two: While visions of sugar-plums danced in their heads;

Group One: And mamma in her 'kerchief, and I in my cap,

Group Two: Had just settled down for a long winter's nap,

Group One: When out on the lawn there arose such a clatter,

Group Two: I sprang from the bed to see what was the matter.

Group One: Away to the window I flew like a flash,

Group Three: Tore open the shutters and threw up the sash.

Group One: The moon on the breast of the new-fallen snow

Group Two: Gave the luster of mid-day to objects below,

Group One: When, what to my wondering eyes should appear,

Group Two: But a miniature sleigh, and eight tiny reindeer,

Group One: With a little old driver, so lively and quick,

Group Two: I knew in a moment it must be St. Nick.

Group Four: More rapid than eagles his coursers they came,

Group One: And he whistled, and shouted, and called them by name;

Group Three: "Now, Dasher! now, Dancer! now, Prancer and Vixen!

Group Four: On, Comet! on Cupid! on Donder and Blitzen!

Group One: To the top of the porch! to the top of the wall!

Group Two: Now dash away! dash away! dash away all!"

Group Three: As dry leaves that before the wild hurricane fly,

Group One: When they meet with an obstacle, mount to the sky,

Group Two: So up to the house-top the coursers they flew,

Group Four: With the sleigh full of toys, and St. Nicholas too.

Group Three: And then, in a twinkling, I heard on the roof

Group Four: The prancing and pawing of each little hoof.

Group Three: As I drew in my hand, and was turning around,

Group Four: Down the chimney St. Nicholas came with a bound.

Group Three: He was dressed all in fur, from his head to his foot,

Group Four: And his clothes were all tarnished with ashes and soot;

Group Three: A bundle of toys he had flung on his back,

Group Four: And he looked like a peddler just opening his pack.

Group Three: His eyes—how they twinkled! His dimples how merry!

Group Four: His cheeks were like roses, his nose like a cherry!

Group One: His droll little mouth was drawn up like a bow,

Group Two: And the beard of his chin was as white as the snow;

Group One: The stump of a pipe he held tight in his teeth,

Group Two: And the smoke it encircled his head like a wreath;

Group One: He had a broad face and a little round belly,

Group Three: That shook when he laughed like a bowlful of jelly.

Group Two: He was chubby and plump, a right jolly old elf,

Group One: And I laughed when I saw him, in spite of myself;

Group Two: A wink of his eye and a twist of his head,

Group One: Soon gave me to know I had nothing to dread;

Group Two: He spoke not a word, but went straight to his work,

Group One: And filled all the stockings; then turned with a jerk,

Group Three: And laying his finger aside of his nose,

Group Four: And giving a nod, up the chimney he rose;

Group Three: He sprang to his sleigh, to his team gave a whistle,

Group Four: And away they all flew like the down of a thistle.

Group Three: But I heard him exclaim, ere he drove out of sight,

Everyone: "Merry Christmas to all, and to all a good-night."

From *Multi-Grade Readers Theatre: Picture Book Authors and Illustrators* by Suzanne I. Barchers and Charla R. Pfeffinger. Santa Barbara, CA: Teacher Ideas Press/Libraries Unlimited. Copyright © 2009.

From Cartoons to Books

Bill Peet
1915–2002

Summary and Background Information

Bill Peet, born William Peed, author and illustrator, preferred to draw and spend his time outdoors. His gift for drawing was recognized while he was in high school, and he won a scholarship to art school. At the John Herron Institute of Art, he realized he didn't like what he called "organized art" but would rather draw comical pictures. Peet was asked to send in some cartoon action sketches to Walt Disney. He worked with Disney for twenty-seven years, grateful for the work. Finally, he left Disney when his career as an author and illustrator of children's books became his main focus.

Presentation Suggestions

The Narrator and Mrs. Stuart can sit off to one side of the staging area. The cartoon characters can sit on the other side, with the students in the middle. If you do not have enough readers, the students can double by reading the cartoon characters' roles as well. If preferred, have the readers wear nametags with pictures of the cartoon characters.

Introductory and Follow-up Suggestions

Bring in the comics from the Sunday newspapers. Read a few aloud. Then ask:

- How do you think cartoonists get their ideas?

- Do any of these cartoons sometimes appear as movies?

- What animated movies have you seen?

After reading the script, ask:

- Walt Disney Studios did most of the animated films for many years. Do you know the names of other studios? (Pixar, which is now associated with Disney, and Dreamworks Animation, may be familiar to the students.)

- How is a cartoon different from other art?

Characters

Grade One: Brooke, Allison, Merlin the Magician

Grade Two: Mrs. Stuart, Kent, Amanda, Crystal, Craig, Elliot, Pinocchio, Dumbo, Bear, Hubert

Grade Three: Narrator, Dwayne, Gordon, Duck, Dalmatian

From Cartoons to Books

Narrator: Mrs. Stuart has asked her students to do a report on Bill Peet. He was an author and an illustrator. He created thirty-five children's books.

Mrs. Stuart: I think you are going to enjoy today's report. Brooke, is your group ready?

Brooke: We have been asked to tell you about Bill Peet. He was an author and an artist.

Kent: Bill Peet was born William Peed. When he started writing books, he changed his name to Bill Peet.

Amanda: He grew up near Indianapolis. He would go up to the attic to draw when he wanted to be alone.

Dwayne: He loved drawing so much that he always had a sketchbook with him. Sometimes he would sneak in some drawing at school. And that got him into trouble at times.

Allison: But he also liked to hike in the country with his friends.

Crystal: He grew up during World War I. He lived near the railroad tracks and watched flatcars rumble by their house.

Craig: He went to art school when he was old enough. He liked to draw cartoon-like pictures. He didn't like to do what he called "organized art."

Crystal: Before he wrote books, he worked for Walt Disney.

Allison: He drew storyboards. They were used to make movies.

Elliot: A storyboard is a set of sketches. They are drawn to tell the story.

Brooke: Soon his job was going well. He married a woman named Margaret.

Kent: They had two sons, Bill and Steve. Mr. Peet would make up stories to tell them at bedtime, which helped his work at Disney.

Amanda: He used his drawings to help with the story lines.

Gordon: He worked on animated features for Mr. Disney. He was one of the very best.

Craig: He enjoyed being creative at his job.

Gordon: He worked on a lot of movies that we have seen. We have asked some of the characters from his movies to visit us. They are going to tell you about his work.

Duck: I was the first character Bill drew and drew and drew. He drew me so many times that he got tired of drawing me. One day he stormed out of the studio screaming, "No more ducks."

Pinocchio: Bill did storyboards for my movie. He was a sketch artist. He worked on my movie for one and a half years. None of his storyboards were used in the movie.

Dumbo: Bill Peet drew me in 1941. He said my cuddly shape was like the shape of his baby boy. He made me famous.

Dalmatian: He retold the story of The *101 Dalmatians*. He also did the sketches. This was the first time he wrote a story and how he started his writing career.

Merlin the Magician: It was Bill's idea to retell the *Sword in the Stone*. I have a bad temper and I like to argue a lot. So did Mr. Disney. I even have his unusual nose. Do you think there is a connection?

Bear: I am in *The Jungle Book*. This is the last movie Peet worked on for Disney. He left before the movie was done to work on his children's books.

Hubert: I am the reason Bill went out on his own. I am the lion in his first book, *Hubert's Hair-Raising Adventure*. I was a great success. Why would Bill need to keep working for Disney now?

Kent: Now Bill could create his own stories and draw things his way. He no longer had to answer to Disney.

Allison: Mr. Peet thought about the stories he had told his sons. They liked them a lot. So he decided to publish them.

From *Multi-Grade Readers Theatre: Picture Book Authors and Illustrators* by Suzanne I. Barchers and Charla R. Pfeffinger. Santa Barbara, CA: Teacher Ideas Press/Libraries Unlimited. Copyright © 2009.

Dwayne: Mr. Peet liked to write about animals. He had spent a lot of time on his grandfather's farm as a child. He would see many animals in the woods.

Elliot: He would go to the zoo and sketch the animals there.

Dwayne: He also loved the circus animals. That's why his favorite book was *Chester the Worldly Pig*. Of course he drew lots of people, too.

Kent: And now we will finish by inviting you to visit Mr. Peet through his books. We like them, and we think you will, too.

A Woman with Tales to Tell

Beatrix Potter

1866–1943

Summary and Background Information

Beatrix Potter grew up in a privileged household in the Lake District of the United Kingdom. Isolated from other children and educated by a governess, she devoted herself to drawing. She became a knowledgeable naturalist but was not allowed to pursue formal study. When she persisted in her search for a publisher, she met and fell in love with Norman Warne, part of Frederick Warne & Company. He died shortly after they became engaged, and she devoted herself to developing her books. She began to acquire land with her royalties and eventually married the lawyer who was assisting her. They moved to one of her properties, Hill Top, and later bought and moved to a large sheep farm. She bequeathed her vast land holdings to the Lake District National Trust, where one can visit her home at Hill Top. For more information, see: http://www.lake-district.gov.uk/.

Presentation Suggestions

The narrators can stand to one side. Beatrix can be on a stool, with Peter and Benjamin on short chairs in front of her. The other characters can stand or sit on chairs. For younger children, consider decorating the area with stuffed animals that might be found in a garden or forest.

Introductory and Follow-up Suggestions

Share a map of the United Kingdom and point out the Lake District, just to the north and west of Manchester. Tell students that this script is about a woman who grew up in Victorian England during the reign of Queen Victoria, 1837 to 1901. Then ask:

- What do you think it was like for women in the 1800s? Do you think they had many choices in their lives?

- What did rich people do? What did poor people do? What did working-class people do?

Students may have no idea what life was like at this time. You can prompt speculation on the life by mentioning that many poor children worked in mines or factories after they turned eight years old. After reading the script, ask:

- What kind of person was Beatrix Potter? What kind of personality did she have?

- How is life different today for most women?

Characters

Grade One: Bertram Potter, Benjamin

Grade Two: Beatrix Potter, Peter, Mrs. Potter, Mr. Potter, Harold Warne, Norman Warne

Grade Three: Narrator One, Narrator Two, Governess

A Woman with Tales to Tell

Narrator One: Beatrix Potter, age ten, lives with her parents and brother in England. Like many young girls in the 1870s, she doesn't go to school. She is taught at home by a governess. Her brother Bertram and her pets are her only friends. Beatrix is in the garden when Bertram runs out to talk with her.

Bertram Potter: Beatrix! Guess what! I'm going to go to boarding school this fall. There will be teachers, and I'll live right at the school! Won't that be grand?

Beatrix Potter: You are so lucky! I would love to go to boarding school, but I know what Mummy and Daddy would say. "You're a girl, Beatrix. Girls stay home with their family. Girls are taught by a governess."

Bertram Potter: I wish you were a boy so you could go to school, too.

Beatrix Potter: Well, there's nothing we can do about that! I guess I'll just have to talk to Benjamin and Peter from now on.

Bertram Potter: But they are rabbits! They can't talk with you.

Beatrix Potter: You just think they don't talk because you don't hear them. They actually have plenty to say.

Bertram Potter: If you say so, Beatrix . . . . Oh! I almost forgot! We need to help pack our things for summer holiday. Let's get back to the house before we get in trouble.

Narrator Two: A few months later, the Potter family is home again. Bertram is at boarding school. Beatrix sits in the garden. She practices drawing her pet rabbits. She talks with them—and it seems to her that they are talking, too.

Beatrix Potter: Benjamin, you are such a rascal. How can I draw a picture of you if you won't sit still? I can't get your back legs quite right when you hop all around like that.

From *Multi-Grade Readers Theatre: Picture Book Authors and Illustrators* by Suzanne I. Barchers and Charla R. Pfeffinger. Santa Barbara, CA: Teacher Ideas Press/Libraries Unlimited. Copyright © 2009.

Benjamin: What do you mean, sit still? I can't find something to eat if I just sit around. Why don't you draw a picture of Peter? He's not doing much of anything.

Peter: I'll have you know I'm busy! I'm watching for that gardener. If he comes back and finds you eating, then we're in trouble.

Benjamin: A likely story! You're just sitting in the sun. Once I find some food, you'll be eating with me.

Beatrix Potter: Now, boys, stop fussing. The gardener is having lunch at the house.

Mrs. Potter: Beatrix! Who are you talking with? Why aren't you at the house for lunch? Young lady, I don't know what I'm going to do with you. You're art is wonderful. But you should be learning useful skills too, such as needlepoint.

Beatrix Potter: Oh, Mother, needlepoint would bore me to tears. Look at this picture of Benjamin. I think it's one of my best rabbit drawings ever. I can't wait to show it to Father.

Mrs. Potter: Yes, it's lovely dear. But you can't live outside drawing. After lunch you need to get to work on your *real* lessons with your governess.

Narrator One: After lunch, Beatrix opens her book and yawns.

Governess: Beatrix, I know you would rather be outside. Let's get this lesson done quickly. Then we will take a walk and look for interesting things to draw.

Beatrix Potter: Could we look for mushrooms? They are easier to draw than rabbits. They aren't moving around all the time!

Governess: Mushrooms may seem easy to draw. Still, there are so many different kinds. Why don't you focus on how each one is unique? You'll have a useful record when you're done.

Beatrix Potter: That's a grand idea! Maybe someday I could do a book about them!

Narrator Two: Beatrix grows up going to museums and practicing her drawing. She loves science. She wants to study at the Royal Botanic Gardens. But women are not allowed. Her parents want her to take over the management of their home. Beatrix wants to do more than that.

Mr. Potter: Beatrix, you need to settle down and help more at home.

Beatrix Potter: But Father, you can hire a housekeeper for that. It is boring. I want to learn more. Someday I want to illustrate a book.

Mr. Potter: Don't be foolish, Beatrix. You will manage this house until you get married. Then you will be prepared to manage your own home.

Narrator One: Beatrix stays home, but she continues to draw. When she is twenty-six years old, she draws animals for a book called *A Happy Pair*. She just uses her initials on the book instead of her name. Few people know that she did the drawings.

Narrator Two: Three years later she writes to the son of a former governess. He is very sick, and Beatrix wants to cheer him up. So she writes and draws a story about a rabbit named Peter. She shows the story to some friends. They tell her to make the story into a book.

Narrator One: At first, no one wants to publish *The Tale of Peter Rabbit*. So Beatrix has her own books made. A few years later, she meets with Harold Warne, a publisher.

Harold Warne: Beatrix, we like your story. But it needs to be in color. Can you illustrate the book in color?

Beatrix Potter: Of course I can! Thank you so much!

Harold Warne: You're welcome. Now, I'd like to meet my brother, Norman. He'll be your editor. He can answer any questions you have.

Narrator Two: *The Tale of Peter Rabbit* is a big hit. Beatrix works with Norman on other books. By 1905, they have fallen in love.

From *Multi-Grade Readers Theatre: Picture Book Authors and Illustrators* by Suzanne I. Barchers and Charla R. Pfeffinger. Santa Barbara, CA: Teacher Ideas Press/Libraries Unlimited. Copyright © 2009.

Norman Warne: Beatrix, I want to speak to your father about us. It is time that we get married and have our own home.

Beatrix Potter: Let me prepare them first.

Narrator One: Beatrix tells her parents about her plans. She is surprised at their reaction.

Mrs. Potter: Oh, Beatrix. I don't think this marriage is a good idea.

Beatrix Potter: Why not?

Mr. Potter: He's just a tradesman, my dear. He works for a publisher.

Beatrix Potter: I love Norman very much. I plan to marry him, with or without your blessing.

Narrator Two: Sadly, Norman dies before their wedding. Beatrix sets aside her sadness. She writes more successful books. She is able to buy her own farm and calls it Hill Top.

Narrator One: Beatrix falls in love again. After getting married, she and William move to Hill Top. Later they move to a large sheep farm.

Narrator Two: Beatrix never has children. But she has many animal friends on their farm. She also buys many pieces of land and farms. When she dies, she leaves her land to the Lake District National Trust in the United Kingdom. If you visit, walk to her house at Hill Top. If you're lucky, you might see a descendant of Peter or Benjamin!

Making Magic

William Steig

1907–2003

Summary and Background Information

William Steig grew up in New York City. He had fond memories of lamplighters lighting the lamps, people sitting out on the stoops at night, and gypsies roaming the streets. As a child, he loved Grimm's fairy tales, Charlie Chaplin movies, and Pinocchio. He was extremely gifted and graduated from high school at age fifteen. He was an accomplished water polo player who had given up the sport to support his family during the Great Depression. The first year he sent some of his cartoons to magazines, he made $4,000. When a friend started a publishing company, he was asked to illustrate *Roland the Minstrel Pig*. At age sixty, he started a new career, writing and illustrating children's books. When he died in 2003, he had written or helped illustrate more than thirty books. One of his final books, *Shrek,* inspired a series of successful children's movies.

Presentation Suggestions

The characters can be sitting casually as if having a conversation while watching the Academy Awards on television. William Steig should be seated centrally.

Introductory and Follow-up Suggestions

Ask students to name their favorite animated film. List the films on the board. Then ask:

- Sometimes the books we read are made into movies. Were any of these films books first?
- How many of you have read the book *Shrek?*
- Who is the author?
- What other books has William Steig written?

After reading the script, list the ten books represented in the script. They are: *Shrek, The Amazing Bone, Brave Irene, Dr. DeSoto, Abel's Island, Farmer Palmer's Wagon Ride, Amos and Boris, Sylvester and the Magic Pebble, Pete's a Pizza,* and *Caleb and Kate.* Reread *Shrek.* Then ask:

- What are some of the differences in the movie and the book? (The introduction of the fairy-tale creatures; Fiona is an ogre in the book but a woman and then an ogre in the movie; Shrek is bald; Lord Farquaad is not in the book.)
- What effect do these changes have on the movie, if any?

Characters

Grade One: Shrek, Sylvester, Pearl, Announcer

Grade Two: Irene, Doctor DeSoto, Abel, Amos, Farmer Palmer, Pete

Grade Three: Narrator, William Steig, Caleb

Making Magic

Narrator: William Steig waits for the Academy Awards to begin on television. He wrote the book *Shrek*. It may win an Oscar for best animated film. Shrek and many of Steig's book friends are with him. They talk with him about their books while they wait.

Shrek: I am so nervous! Just think! First I was in a book. Then I was part of a film. Now I am famous. It's all because of you, William.

William Steig: It's hard to believe, isn't it? I had no idea children would love an ugly ogre like you so much, Shrek!

Shrek: My life had lots of surprises. I met a knight in shining armor. I met a dragon. I met a witch. And I met my true love! I'm glad you wrote about me, William.

Sylvester: Did you always write books for kids, William?

William Steig: No, first I drew cartoons. I did that for a long time. In fact I was sixty years old before I started writing and illustrating children's books.

Sylvester: Did you like to draw when you were a kid?

William Steig: Yes, I did. But I really wanted to be a water polo player!

Irene: You'd have to be really brave to be a water polo player! Were you good at it?

William Steig: I was pretty good, but I had to go to work. My family was poor, and I needed to make money.

Irene: I know what that is like. Sometimes it takes bravery just to help out.

From *Multi-Grade Readers Theatre: Picture Book Authors and Illustrators* by Suzanne I. Barchers and Charla R. Pfeffinger. Westport, CT: Teacher Ideas Press/Libraries Unlimited. Copyright © 2009.

William Steig: That's true, Irene. I enjoyed making cartoons, so I didn't mind helping out and I made pretty good money at it. Then a friend suggested that I try doing a children's book. I discovered that was even *more* fun! Even though we were poor, I had fun growing up. So now I could be like a kid again myself!

Doctor DeSoto: I've always wanted to ask you a question. You have several books with mice in them. Why did you do so many books with mice?

Abel: I've wanted to know that too. Was it because we are so much fun to draw? Because we're so clever? Or because we're so good looking?

Amos: I think I know why you use mice a lot. Mice are small animals, and these mice had big problems to solve. So they had to be smart—incredibly smart!

William Steig: Well, what do you think? Is Amos right?

Doctor DeSoto: I think he is. If Mrs. DeSoto and I hadn't come up with our plan to outwit the fox, we wouldn't be here today.

Abel: I had to learn many lessons so I could get back home.

Amos: Just think how smart a mouse has to be to rescue a whale!

William Steig: Children often feel little—just like a mouse. Maybe the children who read my books feel a bit smarter or braver.

Pearl: You seem to like pigs, too. Why is that?

Farmer Palmer: Wait! I think I know why. It's not because we are little and cute, Pearl! It's because we like to go on journeys and adventures!

Pearl: I do like a good adventure. But I don't like being scared by a fox who thinks I'd be delicious to eat.

Farmer Palmer: But that's what makes the book so exciting. Right, William?

William Steig: You're right about that. A story has to have some suspense. And to be satisfying, it needs a happy ending too.

From *Multi-Grade Readers Theatre: Picture Book Authors and Illustrators* by Suzanne I. Barchers and Charla R. Pfeffinger. Santa Barbara, CA: Teacher Ideas Press/Libraries Unlimited. Copyright © 2009.

Sylvester: I'm glad you like happy endings. Thank goodness for magic, or I might not be here.

William Steig: Oh, I would have thought of something to save you! Sometimes love and faith can be just as magical.

Pete: My story didn't have magic. And it didn't have animals.

William Steig: You're right about the animals, Pete. But I think there was a lot of magic.

Pete: What do you mean? There was nothing magical like a pebble or bone.

William Steig: You were in a pretty bad mood at the beginning of the story. By the end of the story, you were in a pretty good mood. Some readers would think that is magical. Don't you think love has some magic in it?

Caleb: I know what it means to have love and magic in a story.

William Steig: You sure do, Caleb!

Caleb: Why do you write and draw so many animals?

William Steig: They can act just like people without being too scary. And they can make children laugh at the same time. Besides that, they are really fun to draw. Wait a second. I think they are about ready to announce the winner for best animated film.

Narrator: William and his friends hold their breath and listen.

Announcer: And the Oscar goes to . . . *Shrek!*

Narrator: Everyone cheers, with Shrek the loudest of all.

Shrek: Thank you, thank you, William. This is the best day of my life!

William Steig: Thanks to *all* of you! You've made my life richer through your stories. Who wants to celebrate with some popcorn?

Everyone: I do!

Narrator: Now it's your turn to get into the act. William's friends came from ten books. Can you name them?

From *Multi-Grade Readers Theatre: Picture Book Authors and Illustrators* by Suzanne I. Barchers and Charla R. Pfeffinger. Santa Barbara, CA: Teacher Ideas Press/Libraries Unlimited. Copyright © 2009.

What Is Your Name Spelled Backwards?

Lynd Kendall Ward

1905–1985

Summary and Background Information

As a young child, Lynd Ward spent hours looking at pictures in the two books his Methodist minister father allowed him to have. Those pictures took on a life of their own for this young boy who was so ill that he was confined to a home in the Canadian wilderness. When Lynd's health improved, the family moved back to the United States. Lynd's father's socialist activites had a profound effect on him. It has been suggested that Lynd Ward was an active communist at one time. Regardless of his political upbringing, his wood carvings and books have captured acclaim over the years. In this script, the readers learn about the child who became a great illustrator of children's picture books.

Presentation Suggestions

The narrators should sit to one side of the other readers.

Introductory and Follow-up Suggestions

Show students how close Illinois and Canada are on a map. Show students examples of wood carvings and discuss how they are made. Then ask:

- Where is Canada?

After reading the script, ask:

- When Lynd Ward was born he was very sick. Why do you think a doctor would tell his parents to go to Canada so he could get well?

- How do you think Lynd felt living far away in the woods in Canada?

- How would you spend your days if you lived like he did?

- When Lynd Ward was well, his family moved back to Chicago. In first grade, he wrote his name Ward backwards. His name spelled his future job.

- Write your last name backwards. Does it tell you anything? Try this with your first name.

Characters

Grade One: Joyce, Tom, Elaine

Grade Two: Allyson, Terry, José, Jasper, April, Candy

Grade Three: Narrator One, Mrs. Phillips, Narrator Two

What Is Your Name Spelled Backwards?

Narrator One: Mrs. Phillips is talking to her class about Lynd Kendall Ward. He was born in Illinois. He was very sick as a baby, and their doctor said he would get well if they moved north to Canada. Mrs. Phillips has started class so let's listen in.

Mrs. Phillips: The Wards lived by a big woods. There were lots of animals there. Lynd Ward loved watching them.

Joyce: Why didn't he watch TV?

Mrs. Phillips: They didn't have any TVs when Lynd was a child.

Allyson: What else did he do while he lived in the woods?

Mrs. Phillips: He drew a lot.

Terry: What did he draw?

Mrs. Phillips: Things he saw in the woods. Lynd Ward loved to draw. Sometimes his father would let him draw rather than do his chores.

Tom: I wish my father would let me draw rather than do my chores.

Mrs. Phillips: Lynd Ward drew so much that it led to a job.

José: When did Lynd Ward decide to make drawing his job?

Mrs. Phillips: When he was in first grade.

Joyce: Why did he decide that in first grade?

Mrs. Phillips: Lynd Ward wrote the letters of his last name backwards.

Narrator Two: Now, I just have to stop everything right here! Do you know what word he saw when he wrote Ward backwards? He saw the word "draw"!

Mrs. Phillips: He knew it was a sign that he was to always draw.

Terry: How did he make money drawing?

From *Multi-Grade Readers Theatre: Picture Book Authors and Illustrators* by Suzanne I. Barchers and Charla R. Pfeffinger. Santa Barbara, CA: Teacher Ideas Press/Libraries Unlimited. Copyright © 2009.

Mrs. Phillips: He started by doing woodcarvings. Then he drew pictures for books.

Jasper: What was his first book for children?

Mrs. Phillips: His first book for children was *The Biggest Bear.*

Tom: What was the book about?

Candy: I know what the story is about. Can I tell the story?

Mrs. Phillips: Sure, Candy, go ahead.

Candy: The story is about Johnny Orchard. He goes into the woods to shoot a big bear.

Jasper: Wow, he wanted to kill a bear! Why would he want to kill a bear?

Candy: He wanted his family to have a bearskin on the side of their barn. Other people had one. He wanted their barn to look like the other barns.

April: Candy, please tell me that he didn't kill a bear for its skin.

Candy: Johnny didn't kill a bear, but he found a bear cub and brought it home.

José: What would he do with a bear cub?

Tom: I bet he made it his pet.

Candy: Yes, but soon there was a really big problem. Can you guess what it was?

Jasper: I know. The bear got really, really big!

Terry: And I bet it kept getting into trouble.

Candy: You're both right. Now Johnny has an enormous bear at his house. What do you do with an enormous bear?

Elaine: Let it go?

Candy: No, it wouldn't survive after being a pet.

Elaine: Put it in a zoo!

Candy: Yes, and that is just what Johnny Orchard did.

April: What a great idea! He could still see the bear whenever he wanted to.

Allyson: That's a great story.

Mrs. Phillips: You know, children, those pictures were not easy for Mr. Ward to draw. He didn't like the first ten pictures he drew.

Jasper: What did he do with them?

Mrs. Phillips: He threw them out and started all over. Mr. Ward won an award for the illustrations in *The Biggest Bear*. His book won the 1953 Caldecott Medal.

Terry: What other books did he draw pictures for?

Mrs. Phillips: He drew the pictures for *The Little Red Lighthouse and the Great Gray Bridge*. He also did a book all in pictures with no words. It is called *The Silver Pony*.

April: I don't understand. How could you read a book without any words?

Mrs. Phillips: You look at the drawings very carefully to see what they say.

José: That's like being a detective! What did the silver pony do?

Mrs. Phillips: The pony flew through the sky. There was a lonely boy who dreamed he was flying on the silver pony. Then he didn't feel so lonely. The little boy started to think his dream was real and told his father he was riding on a silver pony.

Allyson: Did his father believe him?

Mrs. Phillips: No.

Joyce: How did Lynd show that in a picture?

Mrs. Phillips: He drew a picture of the boy getting spanked.

Tom: Did the dreams stop?

Mrs. Phillips: No, he still had the dreams, but he kept them a secret.

Terry: Are you going to tell us about *The Little Red Lighthouse and the Great Gray Bridge*?

From *Multi-Grade Readers Theatre: Picture Book Authors and Illustrators* by Suzanne I. Barchers and Charla R. Pfeffinger. Santa Barbara, CA: Teacher Ideas Press/Libraries Unlimited. Copyright © 2009.

Mrs. Phillips: Not today, Terry, because we are out of time. I have a good idea, though. Why don't you read the book and you can tell us about it the next time we meet?

Terry: I can do that. Do you have a copy?

Narrator One: Of course Mrs. Phillips had a copy. Maybe your librarian or teacher has a copy of *The Little Red Lighthouse and the Great Gray Bridge*? It's a great book!

From Clowning to the Caldecott

David Wisniewski

1953–2002

Summary and Background Information

David Wisniewski was born in Middlesex, England, during his father's service in the United States Air Force. After several moves, David attended one semester at the University of Maryland. He decided to go to Ringling Brothers and Barnum and Bailey's Clown College and then worked in the circus for three years. He applied for a job with a puppetry theatre, later marrying Donna Harris, the woman who hired him. Having a young family prompted David to search for alternative ways to use his talents to make a living. He began a successful children's book writing and illustrating career, utilizing his experience with puppetry and staging as he made his detailed paper-cut illustrations. *The Golem* won the Caldecott Medal in 1997. David died at age forty-nine after a brief illness.

Presentation Suggestions

The narrators, Mrs. Wisniewski, Mr. Wisniewski, and Donna can stand on one side of David. The other readers can stand on the other side of him. If preferred, the stage can be decorated with circus posters or clowning paraphernalia.

Introductory and Follow-up Suggestions

Share books or photos about the circus. Then ask:

- Have you been to the circus?

- What was your favorite part, or what do you think you'd like to see?

- How do you think clowns learn how to be clowns?

After reading the script, share that the Clown College closed in 1998. Then ask:

• If you could take clowning classes, what would you want to learn to do?

Explain that the American Library Association has a committee of librarians that choose the winners for the Caldecott Medal (for illustrations) and Newbery Medal (for writing). Share other books that have won the Caldecott Medal and have students discuss what makes an award-winning book. Then have students study the illustrations in one of Wisniewski's books. If possible, collaborate with an art teacher and have the students create illustrations using cut paper.

Characters

Grade One: Mrs. Wisniewski, Mr. Wisniewski, Donna Harris, Dorothy Briley

Grade Two: David Wisniewski, Friend, Editor

Grade Three: Narrator One, Narrator Two, Recruiter, Librarian

From Clowning to the Caldecott

Narrator One: David, who is in first grade, likes school. But he likes reading comic books even more, and he wants to be an artist.

Mr. Wisniewski: David, it's time to go to school. Put away your comic books.

David Wisniewski: Okay, Dad. I wish I could draw pictures like the ones in my comic books.

Mrs. Wisniewski: I can help you, David. After school I'll show you how to do some simple figures. You'll be drawing like that in no time!

Narrator Two: David's mother shows him how to use ovals and circles to make men. By third grade, he is one of the best artists in class. By the time David goes to high school, he has become a good actor, too.

Narrator One: David goes to college to study drama. But soon his money runs out. He hears about a free college. David talks to the recruiter.

David Wisniewski: Tell me about this college.

Recruiter: It's a great college for learning all about being a clown.

David Wisniewski: A clown! What kinds of things would I learn?

Recruiter: You'll learn about things like how to put on clown makeup. You'll also learn how to juggle and how to fall down.

David Wisniewski: What does it cost to attend?

Recruiter: You only have to pay for your room and meals. If you get accepted, you have a good chance of getting a job in the circus.

David Wisniewski: Tell me how to apply . . . .

Narrator Two: David gets accepted to Clown College. He tells his parents about his plans.

David Wisniewski: Mom, I just can't afford college, so I'm going to drop out.

Mrs. Wisniewski: I'm sorry, David. I wish things were better. Are you going to get a job?

David Wisniewski: No, I have a better idea. You know how I love to perform and how I love to make people laugh.

Mr. Wisniewski: Of course we do. You're very good at performing and at drawing. You'll be good at whatever you choose to do.

David Wisniewski: Well, this may surprise you. I've tried out for Ringling Brothers and Barnum and Bailey's Clown College. I was accepted.

Mrs. Wisniewski: You were? How will you pay for it?

David Wisniewski: It's free because a lot of the clowns are getting older. The circus will need new clowns, so they are training them. I may end up with a job, too.

Mr. Wisniewski: I think that is great! You'll make a fine clown!

Narrator One: After Clown College, David works with them for two years. Then he works with Circus Vargas for a year. He gets tired of traveling and goes to work for a puppet theatre.

Narrator Two: Six months later, David marries the woman who hired him. They travel a lot with the puppet theatre. Soon they start a family.

David Wisniewski: Donna, I need to do a job that lets me be home more.

Donna Harris: You are so good at art. You can sell illustrations.

Narrator One: A few years later a friend talks with David about his art.

Friend: David, why don't you make children's books?

David Wisniewski: How would I get started? I don't know any editors.

Friend: There is a class on writing and illustrating children's books. Why don't you go? You might meet an editor there.

Narrator Two: David goes to the class. He meets an editor.

Editor: I think your work is terrific. I'm going to give you the names and phone numbers of some editors that I know. Call and tell them I suggested you contact them. The rest is up to you.

Narrator One: It takes David a long time to find his courage. He finally thinks of a good story. He writes it out and makes a few drawings. Then he meets with Dorothy Briley at a publishing house.

Dorothy Briley: I like your work, David. How long will it take you to finish this book?

David Wisniewski: I'm not sure, but I'll get started right away.

Dorothy Briley: Good! I'm glad you brought it to me.

Narrator Two: David does a lot of research for each story that he writes. He often starts with a legend or a folktale. He cuts paper into detailed shapes for the illustrations. Each one takes patience and hard work.

Narrator One: A few years pass by. David has done several books. One day in January, David gets an exciting phone call.

Librarian: Is this Mr. Wisniewski?

David Wisniewski: Yes, it is.

Librarian: I'm calling to tell you that your book *The Golem* has won the Caldecott Medal. Congratulations! This is a great honor.

David Wisniewski: Oh . . . Thank you so much! Donna! Guess what! *The Golem* has won the Caldecott Medal.

Donna Harris: What great news, David!

Narrator Two: David makes other books and wins other awards. He decides to try writing funny books. That's when he learns that it is easier to be a clown! His book *The Secret Knowledge of Grown-Ups* uses his good sense of humor.

Narrator One: By the time David is forty-nine years old, he has created many fine books for children. Sadly, he becomes sick and dies in his sleep. This talented clown dies too soon.

From *Multi-Grade Readers Theatre: Picture Book Authors and Illustrators* by Suzanne I. Barchers and Charla R. Pfeffinger. Santa Barbara, CA: Teacher Ideas Press/Libraries Unlimited. Copyright © 2009.

Part Two

Grades Two, Three, and Four

The Shoemaker's Son

Hans Christian Andersen

1805–1875

Summary and Background Information

Young Hans Christian Andersen doesn't read well. He's small and unattractive, and his family is poor. He feels like a misfit. He takes refuge from teasing by spending time with his father, who reads aloud to him and encourages his creativity. At age fourteen, Hans has become an accomplished storyteller and singer. He leaves Odense, Denmark, to seek his fortune in the big city of Copenhagen, where he seeks help from a famous ballerina and a theatre director. He's helped with furthering his education and begins achieving success as a writer.

Presentation Suggestions

The narrators and teacher can stand on one side. The children can sit on the floor in front of Hans and his family while they stand in the center. The remaining characters can be on the other side.

Introductory and Follow-up Suggestions

Show students where Odense and Copenhagen are on a map of Denmark. Ask the following questions before reading the script:

- This story takes place more than two hundred years ago. What do you think it was like to live in Denmark then?
- The title tells you that the father is a shoemaker. The mother in the story is a washerwoman. What might those jobs be like in the 1800s?

Read aloud "The Ugly Duckling" before reading the script. Then ask:

- Have you ever felt like you didn't fit in, or have you ever been teased? How did it make you feel?

If preferred, don't reveal the author until after reading the script. Then ask:

- Do you know who the author is in this script?

- Some people say "The Ugly Duckling" is the story of his life. Do you agree? Why or why not?

- Can you think of other fairy tales by Hans Christian Andersen that are hinted at in the script? ("The Conceited Apple Branch," "The Emperor's New Clothes," "The Red Shoes," and "The Little Match Girl") Children may think of other tales with similar themes, such as those by the Grimm Brothers. Discuss the similarities. Note that the Grimm Brothers' stories are of the oral tradition, whereas Andersen wrote his, and they are thus called literary tales.

Characters

Grade 2: Father, Child One, Child Two, Child Three

Grade 3: Hans, Children, Teacher, Sister, Madame Schall, Giuseppe Siboni

Grade 4: Narrator One, Narrator Two, Mother, Theatre Director

The Shoemaker's Son

Narrator One: Hans is six years old. He lives with his father, mother, and older sister. They live in a house in Odense, Denmark. His father is a shoemaker, and his mother is a washerwoman. Hans watches the snow falling outside.

Father: Hans, come over here. I've made something just for you.

Hans: A paper snowflake! It's beautiful, Father! Please show me how to make one.

Father: First, take a white piece of paper and fold it over like this and then like that. Next, watch how I use the scissors to make cuts in the paper. Then just unfold it.

Hans: Can we make cutouts of other things?

Father: Of course we can. Here's some more paper for snowflakes. While you are working on them, I'll read aloud to you.

Hans: Can you read the next story in *A Thousand and One Nights* to me? I love hearing you read aloud, Father, but I wish I could read it myself. Reading is just so hard.

Father: Someday you'll be a good reader, Son. You just need to keep trying.

Narrator Two: The next day Hans trudges off to school in the snow. He struggles with reading, so he spends most of his time dreaming up stories. He's one of the smallest and poorest children in the school. This makes Hans a target for teasing and bullying.

Children: Little bitty Hans! Little bitty Hans! No taller than my knee. No bigger than a flea. Little bitty Hans! Little bitty Hans!

Teacher: Children, stop teasing! Hans, come back into the classroom and look at a book.

Narrator One: Hans stays in the classroom as much as he can during the day. He hates the walk home because there is no teacher to stop the teasing.

From *Multi-Grade Readers Theatre: Picture Book Authors and Illustrators* by Suzanne I. Barchers and Charla R. Pfeffinger. Santa Barbara, CA: Teacher Ideas Press/Libraries Unlimited. Copyright © 2009.

Child One: Hans, Hans, Hans! The shoemaker's son. Does he have buckles on his boots? No, he has none! Hans, Hans, Hans! The shoemaker's son.

Child Two: Hans, Hans, Hans! The washerwoman's son. Does he have buttons on his clothes? No, he has none! Hans, Hans, Hans! The washerwoman's son.

Child Three: Hans, Hans, Hans! The shoemaker's son. Can't read or write. Can't even do his sums. Hans, Hans, Hans! The shoemaker's son.

Narrator One: As Hans gets close to home, he sees his mother sweeping in front of the house. She hears the children teasing Hans and waves her broom at them.

Mother: Leave my Hans alone, you little brats! Now get away before I blister one of your backsides with this broom!

Narrator Two: Hans slips into the house. He watches out the window as the laughing children run away. He wonders if he'll ever fit in.

Mother: Hans, don't you worry about those brats. Someday you'll show them that you are better than all of them put together.

Hans: But Mother, I am the littlest in the class. I'm ugly, stupid, and I can't learn anything.

Mother: What about all those stories you learn and the puppet plays you make up? Quit fussing and have a bite to eat with your sister. And don't forget that you're going to see your grandmother on Saturday. You can make something out of cloth scraps and show it to her.

Sister: Maybe he should be learning to read, Mother.

Mother: Hans gets enough learning at that school your father sends him to.

Sister: And why do you let him spend so much time with his grandmother? There are so many crazy people in that place.

Hans: I like going there! If I'm not helping grandmother, I get to listen to the women in the spinning room. They tell wonderful stories.

Sister: Stories! Can't you think of anything else?

Narrator One: Father loves Hans's creative puppet shows and stories. Then, when Hans is eleven years old, his father suddenly gets sick and dies. Hans has to go to a school for the poor where he is teased even more. Then things get even worse, and Hans has to go to work in a cloth factory. He leaves that job after a few days. Then he works in a tobacco factory for a while.

Narrator Two: He isn't good at working, but he gets very good at telling stories. He also gets very good at singing. Sometimes he stands in the garden and practices his songs and stories. People listen to him and talk about how talented he is. By the time he is fourteen, he has also fallen in love with the theatre. He makes a big decision.

Hans: Mother, I need to tell you something. I want to go to Copenhagen.

Mother: Whatever for? What will you do in Copenhagen? How will you make any money?

Hans: I shall go on stage, and I shall become famous. It will be hard for a while, but one day you'll see that this is the right decision.

Mother: Well, son, you are talented. Everyone in Odense talks about your singing and your stories. I'll try to find enough money to send you there.

Narrator One: Hans takes a coach to Copenhagen. Then he tries to get a chance to prove himself. First he visits a famous ballerina.

Hans: Madame Schall, may I perform and sing for you? You won't be disappointed.

Narrator Two: Madame Schall is surprised at how young and brave Hans is.

Madame Schall: You have some talent, young man, but I have no work for you.

Narrator One: Hans doesn't give up. He goes to see a famous theatre director.

Theatre Director: Son, you need to go back to school and get a good education.

Narrator Two: Hans was about to run out of money. Then he heard about a new director named Giuseppe Siboni. He went to see him.

Giuseppe Siboni: Son, you have some talent, but you have a lot to learn. You need acting and singing lessons and need to learn German and Latin. But if you are willing to work hard, I will help you.

Narrator One: Hans had his start, but he still had many challenges ahead. Hans studied hard and began writing books and stories. People in other countries liked his books and stories. But it took a long time for his stories to be accepted in Denmark. He often felt like he didn't quite fit in. He felt like that little boy looking through the window at the laughing children.

Narrator Two: Hans was born more than two hundred years ago. Today his stories are read and told by parents and children all over the world. He told his mother that he was going to be famous, and he was right. His father would have been very proud of Hans.

From *Multi-Grade Readers Theatre: Picture Book Authors and Illustrators* by Suzanne I. Barchers and Charla R. Pfeffinger. Santa Barbara, CA: Teacher Ideas Press/Libraries Unlimited. Copyright © 2009.

Bonjour Paris!

Ludwig Bemelmans
1898–1962

Summary and Background Information

Ludwig Bemelmans, born in the Austrian mountains, worked at his uncle's resort as a teenager until an altercation forced him to immigrate to the United States. He worked in New York City hotels, served in the U.S. Army during World War I, and returned to New York City to continue restaurant work. He became interested in writing for children after meeting an editor from Viking. His first book, *Hansi,* was published by Viking in 1934. But his fame became firmly established with the publication of *Madeline* in 1939. This script provides several facts about Ludwig Bemelmans and introduces French cognates.

Presentation Suggestions

The Narrator and Mr. Buffet should stand on one side, with the children arranged as if in a classroom. The reader for Mr. Buffet should practice reading the French words, all cognates: *restaurant, chocolat, dessert, les fruits, une banane, la salade, le menu, le cheque, l'hôtel, la lampe, l'artiste, le dentist, bonjour, au revoir.* There can be additional readers in the Children roles. Although these words vary between grades 1 and 4 and according to *The EDL Core Vocabularies,* they are easy for readers because of the prompts by Mr. Buffet.

Introductory and Follow-up Suggestions

Show Paris, France, on a map or a globe. Then ask:

- Have any of you traveled to Paris? If so, what do you remember most about it?

- Do any of you know of famous things to see in Paris? (Possible answers include the Eiffel Tower, the Seine River, the Louvre, and Notre Dame.)

- What language do most people speak in Paris? Do you know any French words? If so, what are they?

After reading, discuss how we use many words from different languages every day. For examples, see "Words Borrowed from Other Languages" in *The Reading Teacher's Book of Lists,* 5th edition, by Edward B. Fry and Jacqueline E. Kress (Jossey-Bass, 2006).

Characters

Grade 1: Jeremy, Janeka, Charlotte, Pierre, Marie

Grade 2: Louis, Sandra

Grade 3: Mr. Buffet

Grade 4: Narrator

Varying Grades: Children

Bonjour Paris!

Narrator: It is the last school day before winter break. Jeremy and Janeka dash into their third grade class. They run up to their teacher, bursting with excitement.

Jeremy and Janeka: Guess what! We're going to Paris!

Mr. Buffet: Now that is exciting! Paris is one of my favorite cities. My parents still live there. So I visit every summer.

Jeremy: Do you think you can help us get ready?

Janeka: We need to be able to speak some French in three days.

Mr. Buffet: I'm happy that you want to learn French, but I don't think you have to worry. Many people speak English and French, and many of the signs are in English, too.

Jeremy: Our mom said it's better if you know a few words.

Mr. Buffet: She is absolutely right. Let's wait until the whole class arrives for a French lesson. We can start our lesson with a book that takes place in Paris. Can you remember what it is?

Janeka: *Madeline!* I'll get it!

Narrator: Mr. Buffet reads aloud *Madeline.* Then he talks about the man who wrote the story and did the drawings.

Mr. Buffet: Ludwig Bemelmans was born in the Austrian mountains. He came to New York City in 1914 and worked in hotels. He also joined the Army. He kept a journal and drew lots of pictures. He got married in 1935. Guess what his wife's name was?

Children: Madeline!

Mr. Buffet: That's right. They had a daughter named Barbara. They were visiting an island near France. Mr. Bemelmans had a bike accident and had to stay in a hospital. He noticed a crack in the ceiling that looked like a rabbit, and he saw a nun give some soup to a little girl. Different ideas just kept coming together, and soon the book *Madeline* was born. Now, let's talk about French words. Some of you have French names, and they are exactly the same in English.

Charlotte: My name is French, isn't it?

Mr. Buffet: Yes, Charlotte is French, and so are Gabrielle, Marie, Pierre, and Louis. There are many words that are almost exactly the same in both English and French. Let's start with some very important words. I'm going to say the French word, and you repeat it. Then say the English word. *Restaurant.*

Children: *Restaurant.* Restaurant!

Mr. Buffet: See how easy this can be? Now here's a favorite of mine—*chocolat.*

Children: *Chocolat.* Chocolate!

Mr. Buffet: Very good! *Dessert.*

Children: *Dessert.* Dessert!

Mr. Buffet: Here's another easy one in case you don't want to just eat sweets. Pierre, what is *les fruits*?

Pierre: *Les fruits.* Fruit? But what does *les* mean?

Mr. Buffet: It means the same as *the* in English, but it also means more than one fruit. Louis, here's another useful one—*une banane.*

Louis: *Une banane.* That's an easy one, a banana. But what is *une?*

Mr. Buffet: You said it right—a banana. The word *une* is also an article, like our words *a* or *an.* You're catching on. Now you might want to eat *la salade.*

Sandra: *La salade.* That has to mean salad, but can you explain the word *la?*

Mr. Buffet: French has different articles that go with different words. But we don't have time to learn all of the differences. Let's keep going. Here's another easy one—*le menu.*

Marie: *Le menu.* The menu!

Mr. Buffet: When you are all done with your meal, your parents will ask for *le cheque.*

Children: *Le cheque.* The check!

Mr. Buffet: That's right. Here's where you'll probably be staying—at *l'hôtel.*

Children: *L'hôtel.* The hotel!

Mr. Buffet: And when you go in your room, you may want to turn on *la lampe.*

Children: *La lampe.* The lamp!

Mr. Buffet: Let's talk about some words for people. When you are sightseeing, Jeremy, you might see this person—*l'artiste.*

Jeremy: *L'artiste.* An artist?

Mr. Buffet: Let's hope you don't need to see *le dentiste,* Janeka.

Janeka: *Le dentist.* The dentist!

Mr. Buffet: We're almost out of time. Are there some words you would like to learn?

Janeka: How do we say hello?

Mr. Buffet: That's a word you must learn—*bonjour.* Let's all say it.

Children: *Bonjour!*

Mr. Buffet: And now we'll learn how to say goodbye—*au revoir.* Try it.

Children: *Au revoir!*

Mr. Buffet: We are out of time, but there's one more thing I need to say to Janeka and Jeremy. *Bon voyage!* Have a good trip!

Children: *Bon voyage!*

If It's by the Berenstains, It's Got to Be about Bears

Stanley Berenstain

1923–2005

Summary and Background Information

Stanley Berenstain and his wife, Janice, met while they were in college in Philadelphia. When asked who did the writing and who did the drawings in their famous series of books on the lives of the bears, the answer was simple. The one who thought up the idea wrote it all down. Then they each helped organize the words and draw and ink the pictures. They started doing the books because their children liked the Dr. Seuss books. They went to work for Dr. Seuss, and their first book was *The Big Honey Hunt,* published in 1962. At the time of Mr. Berenstain's death, they had published more than 250 books. Today, Janice Grant Berenstain and her sons continue the tradition of writing Berenstain Bears books.

Presentation Suggestions

The narrators and teacher can stand on one side. Kevin should stand facing the other readers, who can sit at an angle on one side.

Introductory and Follow-up Suggestions

Ask the students what books they have read by the Berenstains. Discuss what they remember about the books. Then ask:

- When Mr. and Mrs. Berenstain decided to write children's books, they used bears to present their stories. What other books do you know that have bears in the story? (*Blueberries for Sal* by Robert McCloskey, *Corduroy* by Don Freeman, *Goldilocks and the Three Bears,* etc.)

- Mr. and Mrs. Berenstain used their stories to teach lessons. What lessons do you remember from the Berenstains' books?

After reading the script, ask:

- The Berenstains wrote the Berenstain's Bear books as a series of books for children. When Mr. Berenstain died, how many books do you think were in the Berenstain's Bear series? (250)

- Who do you think is writing the Berenstain books now? (Mrs. Berenstain and her sons)

Characters

Grade Two: Ronnie, Linc, Jake

Grade Three: Kevin, Jackie, Emma, Leah, Anna, Don, Maria, Julia

Grade Four: Narrator, Mrs. Knight

If It's by the Berenstains, It's Got to Be about Bears

Narrator: Kevin is going to tell Mrs. Knight's class about a writer he likes.

Kevin: I often read these books to my little brother. They're all about animals that talk, play, and get into trouble. Their mama and papa have to care for them. The stories are like real life, except that it's about bears. If it's Berenstains' books, it's got to be about bears. What do you think, Mrs. Knight?

Mrs. Knight: I thought you were going to tell us about the bears.

Kevin: First, I want to start by talking about Stanley Berenstain. He was born in Philadelphia, Pennsylvania. His parents knew he could draw well when he was very small.

Jackie: How did his parents know that his pictures were any good?

Kevin: He made an enormous drawing about boxing right on the wall. He drew it in their living room.

Ronnie: I bet his parents were upset with him!

Kevin: I am sure they were. They were a very poor family. When Stan was six years old, the economy was very poor in the United States. There was a depression.

Linc: What do you mean by a depression?

Kevin: It means a lot of people lost their money in the stock market. Many people didn't have jobs. It was a very hard time. In 1941, Stan went to the Philadelphia Museum School of Industrial Art. This is where he met Janice.

Emma: Did he marry Janice?

Kevin: Yes, but first he joined the army. It was during World War II. Everyone who could joined the military.

Leah: Did he have to give up being an artist so he could fight in the army?

Kevin: No, he made drawings for the army doctors.

Ronnie: What kind of drawings would doctors use?

Kevin: He might draw ways to fix wounds to the face or how to sew up bullet holes. Sometimes he'd draw new ideas so there wouldn't be ugly scars.

Mrs. Knight: That is just amazing, Kevin. What a wonderful thing to be able to do for others.

Jackie: It must have been hard to see all those soldiers injured.

Kevin: I'm sure it was, but sometimes he had free time. Then he would draw cartoons and sell them to magazines. After the war, he married Janice. She had been working as a riveter during the war.

Leah: I've read about them. There were women who worked in the factories during the war. They were called "Rosie the Riveters."

Jake: What did the riveters do?

Leah: They would put the rivets into the ships that would be used in the war. Rivets are very sturdy nails.

Kevin: Let me tell you about their writing. Stan and Janice had two sons. Michael and Leo both loved the Dr. Seuss books. Stan and Janice decided to do stories for their boys. They wanted them to be funny stories. But they also wanted them to help kids deal with things that really happen in their lives.

Emma: Was there any special reason why they chose bears?

Kevin: Because they are easy to draw. They could dress them up and make them look like real people. They named them Mama, Papa, Brother, and Sister so it would be easy for kids to remember their names. Their first children's book was *The Big Honey Hunt.* I bet a lot of you have read these books, so I'm going to ask you some questions. First, what did Papa always wear?

Anna: He wore overalls. He also wore a yellow shirt.

Kevin: That's right. What did Mama bear always wear?

Emma: She always wore this silly spotted hat that matched her dress.

Kevin: Why do you think the bears always wore the same kind of clothes in the drawings?

Don: So children could always find them in the pictures.

Kevin: What did Sister wear, and what was her favorite doll?

Julia: Sister had a Bearbie doll. And she always wore a pink bow in her hair and wore pink overalls.

Kevin: Did anyone have a favorite part in the book *Too Much Vacation*?

Jake: Mama was using a new camera. Click, click, click, click, click.

Anna: They had so many problems in that story.

Kevin: Like what?

Anna: The cabin was filthy, and there was no water in the pump.

Julia: When they went out hiking, they picked some berries, but they were sour.

Ronnie: They wanted to watch the sunset. But lots of mosquitoes bit them!

Maria: They finally went home because it rained so much that the roof of the cabin leaked. Mama took pictures of it all!

Don: When they got home they looked at the pictures Mama took. The pictures were so good that they decided they had had a good time after all.

Kevin: Does anyone else have a favorite book?

Maria: I liked the one about Sister and Lizzy. They had a big fight over who was going to be the teacher. When I was little I used to play school. I would be the teacher, just like Lizzy and Sister wanted to be.

Linc: I liked *Trouble at School*. When Brother learned to be honest, good things happened to him.

From *Multi-Grade Readers Theatre: Picture Book Authors and Illustrators* by Suzanne I. Barchers and Charla R. Pfeffinger. Santa Barbara, CA: Teacher Ideas Press/Libraries Unlimited. Copyright © 2009.

Mrs. Knight: What was the most important thing you learned from your research, Kevin?

Kevin: I learned that Mr. Berenstain wanted their books to teach. I also learned that keeping things simple is best.

Mrs. Knight: What do you mean by keeping things simple?

Kevin: The bears always dressed the same. They had names that are easy to remember. Things that happened to them could happen to us. By reading the books, I could learn how to handle myself if I have those same problems some day.

Mrs. Knight: I think that message is a great place to end our discussion of the Berenstains. Thank you, Kevin!

From *Multi-Grade Readers Theatre: Picture Book Authors and Illustrators* by Suzanne I. Barchers and Charla R. Pfeffinger. Santa Barbara, CA: Teacher Ideas Press/Libraries Unlimited. Copyright © 2009.

Trains, Steam Shovels, and Little Houses

Virginia Lee Burton

1909–1968

Summary and Background Information

Virginia Lee Burton spent her early years living in Massachusetts. Her mother was a musician and poet. Her father served as the first dean at the Massachusetts Institute of Technology until he retired in 1921. His retirement prompted a move to Carmel, California, where the family members continued their interest in the arts. Virginia attended art school and eventually moved back east to Boston. There she married George Demetrios, a sculptor and teacher. Their two sons proved to be the inspiration for her children's books, including the Caldecott Medal winner, *The Little House*. Youngsters continue to enjoy *Mike Mulligan and His Steam Shovel* more than sixty years later.

Presentation Suggestions

Place the readers in the following order: Narrator One, Narrator Two, Mrs. Burton, Mr. Burton, Virginia, Mabel, Aris, Jim, Oley, Archibald, and Mike. If read for younger students, add trains and toy construction vehicles to the stage.

Introductory and Follow-up Suggestions

Show students several books by Virginia Lee Burton. Then ask:

- How long ago do you think these books were written?

- How are the illustrations different from or like other books?

Examine the copyright page of each book. Subtract the copyright year from the current year and determine how long ago each book was published. After reading the script, ask:

- What do you know about the years when Virginia Burton was growing up?

- Do you think her sons gave her good advice?

- Do you think her books are still good? Why or why not?

- What advice would you give authors or illustrators today?

Characters

Grade Two: Mr. Burton, Aris, Oley, Mike

Grade Three: Mrs. Burton, Virginia, Narrator Two, Mabel

Grade Four: Narrator One, Jim, Archibald

Trains, Steam Shovels, and Little Houses

Narrator One: Virginia lives with her mother, father, and sister in Newton Center, Massachusetts. Her parents love music and art. The family enjoys living in the northeast for many years. Then Virginia's life changes.

Mrs. Burton: Virginia, your father and I have some exciting news to share with you.

Mr. Burton: I am retiring from being a dean. We want to live someplace warmer. So we are moving.

Virginia: Do we have to move a long ways to be someplace warmer?

Mr. Burton: Yes, we're moving to California.

Mrs. Burton: It is a long way away, but I think you'll like it.

Narrator Two: Virginia does like California. They live in a small town where there are three theaters. Virginia gets to be in plays. She learns to dance and enjoys performing.

Narrator One: When Virginia is in high school, she gets a scholarship to an art school. She loves the classes but doesn't want to go to college. She talks with her friend about her plans for the future.

Virginia: Mabel, I think I want to keep going to art school. I also want to continue studying ballet.

Mabel: Let's move near San Francisco. We can commute to school together.

Narrator Two: The two friends move to a town across the bay from San Francisco. They have to travel by train, ferry, and cable car to get to school. Sometimes the trip takes more than two hours.

Mabel: Virginia, don't you get tired of these long trips to school?

Virginia: Not really. Look at the sketches of people I've made on this trip. Someday perhaps all of this practice will pay off, and someone will pay me for work like this.

Mabel: What kind of artwork would you like to do?

Virginia: I'd like to draw for books, maybe even for children's books. I used to love the books my parents would get me for Christmas. They had such wonderful illustrations. Or maybe I'll become a dancer like my sister.

Narrator Two: Virginia doesn't become a dancer. She returns to the East Coast and goes to art school in Boston. She falls in love with George Demetrios, an artist and teacher. They get married and start a family.

Narrator One: Virginia and George have two sons named Aris and Michael. Virginia loves watching her children play, and she loves drawing while they play.

Narrator Two: She watches Aris play with his trains and has an idea.

Virginia: Aris, you have been playing with that train for hours. Can you tell me what you like best about it?

Aris: The engine is shiny and black, and it goes *choo choo*.

Virginia: What are those other noises you keep making?

Aris: It has a whistle that goes *whoo whoo* and a bell that goes *ding dong*.

Virginia: Does it make a noise when it stops?

Aris: Yes, the brakes go *sssswish* really loud when the train stops.

Virginia: Aris, I'm going to make some drawings of your train while you play. You can keep playing while I work.

Narrator One: Aris's play with his train has inspired Virginia to create a story about a train. When she creates a book, she starts with the illustrations first. Then she works on writing the story. After a while, she shows Aris her drawings.

Virginia: What do you think of these train drawings, Aris? Have I forgotten anything?

From *Multi-Grade Readers Theatre: Picture Book Authors and Illustrators* by Suzanne I. Barchers and Charla R. Pfeffinger. Santa Barbara, CA: Teacher Ideas Press/Libraries Unlimited. Copyright © 2009.

Aris: You need to meet the people on my train, and then you can draw them.

Virginia: Who are they?

Narrator Two: Virginia can hear the train people speaking to her.

Jim: I'm the engineer. I make sure everything works right.

Oley: I'm the fireman. I feed the engine coal and water.

Archibald: I'm the conductor. I take the tickets from the passengers.

Narrator One: Virginia works on her story ideas and tries them out on Aris. Soon she has a story ready to try to publish. *Choo Choo* becomes her first published book. She dedicates it to her son Aris.

Narrator Two: A year or so later, Virginia watches her other son play in his sandbox. Mike pushes a toy steam shovel back and forth.

Mike: We're going to dig a tunnel through the mountains. Then the cars can get through to the city. Then we can help make the new buildings and skyscrapers.

Virginia: Mike, tell me some more about your steam shovel and the work it's doing.

Mike: It's a very busy steam shovel. There is a lot to do when you're digging a tunnel. It's also noisy when it's working. Bing! Bang! Crash! Slam!

Virginia: You've given me a good idea for a story. Some of the new shovels are powered by diesel instead of steam. What if people thought those were better?

Mike: What would all the steam shovels do if they couldn't help build things?

Virginia: That's a good question, and I think that is what the story should be about. I'm going to start working on some drawings while you work on your buildings. I'll get your help later.

Narrator One: Virginia's second book is called *Mike Mulligan and His Steam Shovel.* Maybe you've read it. Mike is named after her son, and the book is dedicated to him. Mike Mulligan proves that his steam shovel can dig a cellar in one day. But then they have a problem to solve when they get stuck in that cellar. Do you remember how they solved the problem?

Narrator Two: Virginia creates seven books for children. *The Little House* wins the Caldecott Medal. She share her ideas and drawings with her sons and their friends. She knows that if they like the books, other children will like them. More than sixty years later, children still love books by Virginia Lee Burton.

A Short Life and a Long Legacy

Randolph Caldecott

1846–1886

Summary and Background Information

Randolph Caldecott was the third child of John Caldecott, an accountant and businessman, and his first wife, Mary Caldecott. Randolph was an excellent student, who left school at age fifteen to work in the field of banking. His true love was illustrating, and he achieved enough sales of his work by the age of twenty-six to feel confident in leaving banking. He married soon after, and he and his wife enjoyed his success. However, his health was precarious, causing them to seek warmer climes in the winters. In January of 1886, they traveled to Florida, hoping to enjoy a warm winter. Instead, he became sick and died suddenly. More than fifty years later, Frederic G. Melcher, a prominent publisher and advocate for children's books, proposed that the American Library Association create a new award that recognized distinguished illustrations in a picture book. The Caldecott Medal is named after Randolph Caldecott in recognition of his contributions to children's book illustrations.

Presentation Suggestions

Narrator One, Narrator Two, John Caldecott, and Mary Caldecott can stand to one side of the stage. Randolph Caldecott and Marian Caldecott can stand in the middle. The other readers can be on the other side of the stage.

Introductory and Follow-up Suggestions

Show the students a variety of books that have the Caldecott Medal award sticker on the book. Then ask:

- Which of these books do you know?

- Each book has an award on the front. What do you know about the award?

After reading the script, share a variety of books that have been published in the past year. Have the students vote on which one they think should win the Caldecott Medal. Share the winning book after it is announced by the American Library Association in January. Then discuss what makes the illustrations distinguished.

Characters

Grade Two: Mary Caldecott, Marian Caldecott, Marguerite Melcher

Grade Three: John Caldecott, Thomas Armstrong, Randolph Caldecott, Frederic G. Melcher

Grade Four: Narrator One, Narrator Two, Edmund Evans

A Short Life and a Long Legacy

Narrator One: John and Mary Caldecott live near Chester, England. The year is 1848. Their son, Randolph, is fourteen years old.

John Caldecott: Mary, we need to talk about Randolph. He spends most of his time outside drawing. You can't make money drawing pretty pictures.

Mary Caldecott: He'll figure out what to do to earn a living. He's only fourteen.

John Caldecott: He's almost an adult, Mary.

Mary Caldecott: I know, but I also know that he's a hardworking young man. You worry too much, dear.

Narrator Two: A year later, Randolph leaves school and begins working at a bank. He lives nearby in a small village. He spends his spare time walking or riding his horse in the countryside.

Narrator One: Randolph is still a teenager when his first drawing is published. The Queen Railway Hotel in Chester is destroyed in a fire. Randolph's drawing of the fire is published in a London newspaper.

Narrator Two: Randolph goes to art school after moving to another bank. He practices his drawings whenever he can. Then he gets some unexpected help from a friend at the bank.

Thomas Armstrong: Randolph, there is someone I want you to meet. Henry Blackburn is the editor of *London Society*. I think they would buy your drawings for the magazine.

Randolph Caldecott: I appreciate the introduction, Thomas. I'd like to show him my work.

Narrator One: Randolph sells several of his drawings to the magazine. By now, he is twenty-six years old. He tells Thomas about a big decision.

Randolph Caldecott: Thomas, I am grateful you introduced me to Mr. Blackburn. I've sold many of my drawings to him. So I am leaving banking. I'm moving to London.

Thomas Armstrong: Congratulations, Randolph! I think you will do very well with your art.

Narrator Two: By the time Randolph is thirty years old, he has received several honors for his work. He makes friends easily. One of those is Edmund Evans, who is a printer.

Edmund Evans: Randolph, would you be willing to illustrate two children's books in time for Christmas? Walter Crane isn't working for me anymore.

Randolph Caldecott: I would very much like illustrating for you. But what are the books about?

Edmund Evans: You'd select the verses and stories and then illustrate them. And if you're a good writer, you could add some writing of your own.

Randolph Caldecott: Let's work out the details, and I'll get started right away.

Narrator One: Randolph's books are very successful. He decides to create two children's books each year. He also decides to get married. A few years later, Randolph tells his wife some important news.

Randolph Caldecott: Marian, my book of nursery rhymes is selling very well. It's selling all around the world.

Marian Caldecott: That is wonderful news. If we don't need to worry about money, then you should rest more. You have been working so hard, and I know you don't feel well much of the time.

Randolph Caldecott: It's these cold London winters that bother me. Let's go to the south of France this winter. We can easily afford it, and we'll both enjoy being near the sea.

Marian Caldecott: That's a great idea. I'll start getting organized for the trip.

Narrator Two: Randolph becomes famous for his drawings. But his health is very poor. In 1886, he and Marian discuss their winter plans.

Randolph Caldecott: What do you think about going to America for the winter?

Marian Caldecott: Where would we go there?

Randolph Caldecott: To Florida, where it is supposed to be very warm in the winter. We'll go by ship to New York and then go south to Florida.

Narrator One: That year happens to be a very cold winter. Randolph gets very sick and dies suddenly in St. Augustine, Florida. He is only thirty-nine years old.

Narrator Two: More than fifty years pass. Randolph Caldecott is still famous for his drawings. He is about to become even more famous.

Narrator One: Frederic G. Melcher is a children's book publisher in the United States. He loves to promote children's books. He talks to his wife about a new idea.

Frederic G. Melcher: I want to start an award that honors children's books.

Marguerite Melcher: What a wonderful idea! Will it be for the writing?

Frederic G. Melcher: No, I think it should be for the illustrations.

Marguerite Melcher: Well, that is what children notice most.

Frederic G. Melcher: And I think it should be named after Randolph Caldecott. He illustrated so many fine children's books.

Narrator Two: The American Library Association awards the first Caldecott Medal in 1938. It is awarded to Dorothy P. Lathrop for her illustrations in *Animals of the Bible, A Picture Book*.

Narrator One: Each year the latest winner is announced in January. And Randolph Caldecott will never be forgotten for his work in children's books.

From *Multi-Grade Readers Theatre: Picture Book Authors and Illustrators* by Suzanne I. Barchers and Charla R. Pfeffinger. Santa Barbara, CA: Teacher Ideas Press/Libraries Unlimited. Copyright © 2009.

Draw to Live and Live to Draw

Wanda Gág

1893–1946

Summary and Background Information

Born to impoverished parents in the late 1800s, Wanda Gág (pronounced gog) was the oldest of seven children. Her father, an artist, died of tuberculosis when Wanda was fifteen. Before he died, he implored her to take care of the family. Because her mother was sick, Wanda took on jobs to keep the family together through the early 1900s and World War I. By the time of the Great Depression, she was beginning to earn money through her art and children's books. *Millions of Cats* won the Newbery Honor Medal, which was unusual for a picture book. The Caldecott Medal for illustrations in pictures books had not yet been established. A lifelong smoker, she died of lung cancer at age fifty-three. This script is presented in a choral reading format, with Responding Readers reading variations on the sentence made famous in *Millions of Cats: Hundreds of cats, thousands of cats, millions and billions and trillions of cats.* Although the readability of this line is Grade 5, the repetitive nature of the lines makes it easier to read.

Presentation Suggestions

Readers One, Two, and Three can be facing the Responding Readers if the whole class is involved. Alternatively, Readers One, Two, and Three can be standing in the back row, with the Responding Readers seated in the front row.

Introductory and Follow-up Suggestions

If you believe that your students are not familiar with *Millions of Cats,* read it aloud to them. Then ask:

- Do you really think that an old man could bring home that many cats?

- What makes this book fun? (Exaggeration, repetition, drawings, etc.)

After reading the script, share other books by Wanda Gág. Then ask:

- How are Wanda Gág's illustrations different from books that are published today?

- Wanda Gág's motto was "Draw to live and live to draw." What does that mean?

Characters

Grade Two: Reader Two

Grade Three: Reader Three

Grade Four: Reader One

Grade Five: Responding Readers

Draw to Live and Live to Draw

Reader One: You have probably heard the book *Millions of Cats.* Do you remember how many cats were in it?

Responding Readers: Hundreds of cats. Thousands of cats. Millions and billions and trillions of cats!

Reader Two: That's right! The story was about an old woman and man who wanted a cat, so the man went out to bring back the prettiest cat. He couldn't decide which one was the prettiest. So he brought back. . . .

Responding Readers: Hundreds of cats. Thousands of cats. Millions and billions and trillions of cats!

Reader Three: Of course the story didn't end there. That is an impossible number of cats to handle!

Reader One: Let's find out about the author, Wanda Gág. She was born in 1893 into a poor family. Her parents, Anton and Lissi, had six more children.

Reader Two: Wanda's father was an artist. But he died when she was fifteen years old. Before he died, he told her to take care of the family. Her mother was sick, too. So Wanda got jobs to keep the family together.

Responding Readers: Hundreds of jobs. Thousands of jobs. Millions and billions and trillions of jobs!

Reader Three: Not *that* many jobs! But she did work hard. She graduated from high school and became a teacher for a year. She also wrote and did illustrations for magazines. She designed a lot of greeting cards.

Responding Readers: Hundreds of cards. Thousands of cards. Millions and billions and trillions of cards!

Reader One: She was busy, that's for sure. She went to art school for a few years. She decided to draw and paint more by 1923. She illustrated books and began making some money from her paintings.

From *Multi-Grade Readers Theatre: Picture Book Authors and Illustrators* by Suzanne I. Barchers and Charla R. Pfeffinger. Westport, CT: Teacher Ideas Press/Libraries Unlimited. Copyright © 2009.

Responding Readers:	Hundreds of dollars. Thousands of dollars. Millions and billions and trillions of dollars!
Reader Two:	Not many writers made that kind of money! But things were good for Wanda. An editor saw her work. She asked Wanda to think about writing for kids.
Reader Three:	*Millions of Cats* came out in 1928. It was an unusual book for kids. But everyone loved it. It won the Newbery Honor Award.
Reader One:	Times were hard during the 1930s. The United States was in a depression. But Wanda kept writing and illustrating. *Snippy and Snappy* was a book about two field mice who wandered away from home.
Reader Two:	Those mice didn't listen to their mother! They got into *big* trouble.
Reader Three:	Wanda liked animals, it seems. She had a success with a book about cats and then about mice.
Responding Readers:	Hundreds of mice. Thousands of mice. Millions and billions and trillions of mice!
Reader One:	One of her books was a family project. Wanda's brother Howard and sister Flavia helped her create *ABC Bunny.*
Responding Readers:	Hundreds of bunnies. Thousands of bunnies. Millions and billions and trillions of bunnies!
Reader Two:	There was just one bunny. But he had a big journey through the alphabet!
Reader Three:	Wanda got married in 1943. She died of lung cancer just three years later. She was only fifty-three years old when she died.
Reader One:	Wanda had one motto or saying about life: Draw to live and live to draw. She lived that motto every day. She never had children, but she created books that were loved and read by millions of readers.
Responding Readers:	Hundreds of readers. Thousands of readers. Millions and billions and trillions of readers!

The Joy and the Agony

Kenneth Grahame

1859–1932

Summary and Background Information

Kenneth Grahame's life was filled with great sorrow and tragedy. His father was an alcoholic who rarely worked. His mother died when he was five years old from scarlet fever. Grahame contracted the disease, and his grandmother came to Scotland to get him and his sibling. He was raised in England for a while in a storybook house with gardens and ponds. These were the best years of his life and are reflected in the description of the areas in his writings, particularly *The Wind and the Willows*. He married and had a son, nicknamed Mouse. Mouse had several birth defects and was a spoiled child who misbehaved badly. He was in and out of boarding schools and finally committed suicide at age twenty by lying on the train tracks. Grahame's belief that it is best to always be a child is a recurrent theme in his writing. In *The Wind and the Willows,* Mr. Toad is considered to be a parallel to his son. The other main characters represent adults who want to change Mr. Toad. This script describes the influences of Grahame's difficult life on his writing.

Presentation Suggestions

The readers should sit in a semicircle with Jeremy and Maria in the center so they can face them when they interact. Narrator One can stand in front of the readers to introduce the script and then leave the staging area. Narrator Two can enter the stage for the final lines. If preferred, each reader could stand during his or her lines.

Introductory and Follow-up Suggestions

Before reading the script, ask:

- Have you ever been sad or lonely? What are some things that made you feel sad or lonely?

- What did you do to escape feeling sad or lonely?

- Who takes care of you when you get sick?

After reading the script, reread selected portions of *The Wind in the Willows* as time allows. Have students identify other evidence of Kenneth Grahame's feelings of agony and joy.

Characters

Grade Two: Claire, Wilma

Grade Three: Jeremy, Maria, Raymond, Edwin, Yolanda, Carolyn, Jess, Stuart

Grade Four: Narrator One, Narrator Two

The Joy and the Agony

Narrator One: Kenneth Grahame had a very hard life. He grew up without the help of loving parents. Jeremy and Maria learned a lot about how Grahame used these experiences when writing. They lead a book talk about him in the library.

Jeremy: Maria and I read *The Wind in the Willows*. Then we learned a lot about the author. His name was Kenneth Grahame. First, Maria will tell you something about Mr. Grahame. You can ask questions at any time.

Maria: Kenneth Grahame was born in Scotland. When he was five years old, his mother died of scarlet fever. He got scarlet fever, too. His father could not take care of him properly. His grandmother came to get him and his baby brother. She took them home with her to England. Grandmother's house was called "The Mount." Around the house were a wild orchard, a terraced garden, and ponds. He said it was like a storybook house.

Claire: Was Toad House like his grandmother's house?

Jeremy: Yes, it was. He said the two years he lived there were the happiest years of his life. He never forgot how wonderful it was there.

Wilma: Why did he live there only two years?

Jeremy: They had to move because the chimney fell down on the house. Uncle John had to find them another place to live. He rented them a smaller house. Kenneth didn't like it as well because it had no gardens.

Raymond: Why didn't his father find the family a place to live?

Maria: Kenneth's father wasn't able to work for a while.

Edwin: Who paid the family's bills if the father didn't work?

From *Multi-Grade Readers Theatre: Picture Book Authors and Illustrators* by Suzanne I. Barchers and Charla R. Pfeffinger. Santa Barbara, CA: Teacher Ideas Press/Libraries Unlimited. Copyright © 2009.

Jeremy: Uncle John helped out until Kenneth's father could take the boys back to Scotland. But things didn't go well, and Kenneth was sent to boarding school when he was nine.

Yolanda: I bet Kenneth didn't think much of his father after he let him down twice.

Maria: You're right. Kenneth decided that he couldn't count on adults.

Wilma: Did he like being at a boarding school?

Maria: The boarding school was a terrible place. The buildings were falling down, and the children saw rats in them. The boys were fed porridge and fatty meat.

Carolyn: What a horrible place to go to school! How did he survive it all?

Jeremy: In his free time, he would walk along the River Thames and pretend things were better. When he finished school, he went to work as a bank clerk.

Jess: Did he want to work in a bank, or did he want to be a writer?

Jeremy: Uncle John got him the bank job, so he had no choice. He began to hate it and would take long vacations or call in sick so that he could travel. He wrote when traveling.

Wilma: Was *The Wind in the Willows* his first book?

Maria: No. He started writing for magazines. Then he wrote a story about five children who spent all their time playing in the garden of their uncle's house.

Stuart: Did he ever get married?

Jeremy: He did, but it was an unhappy marriage. His wife wanted a husband who would stay home. He loved to wander so that he could dream up stories to write.

Jess: Did they have any children?

Maria: They had a son they called Mouse. He was blind in one eye, but he was very smart. They spoiled him rotten, and he became a terrible child, especially with other children. He would even lie down on the road in front of cars when he did not get his way.

Edwin: That sounds like Mr. Toad! Spoiled, selfish, and always wanting his way, even when it was going to hurt him. He'd throw fits and sneak around to do what he wanted. I bet Mr. Grahame used his son as a model for Mr. Toad!

Jeremy: No one knows for sure, but it seems like it. At first, Mr. Grahame told the stories in *The Wind and the Willow*s to his son when he was young. When he was away, he would write additions to the story and send them to Mouse. It was never supposed to be a book.

Raymond: Why did Mr. Grahame make the stories into a book then?

Maria: His agent wanted him to do a new book, and the Grahames needed the money. Then *The Wind and the Willows* became a big success! They put Mouse in a boarding school so they could travel more.

Carolyn: I hope it wasn't a boarding school like the one Mr. Grahame went to.

Maria: Mouse went to fine schools, but it didn't matter. He was never happy and died on his twentieth birthday.

Yolanda: Poor Mr. Grahame.

Claire: He had a sad and lonely life.

Jess: I wonder why he didn't write another book.

Jeremy: He said he didn't have the energy to write more books. He knew people liked his book, but he didn't think readers understood it.

Wilma: What did he mean?

Jeremy: He said that readers didn't see the agony or the joy in his book.

Stuart: I didn't think there was agony in the book. The animals made some bad decisions.

Edwin: I haven't read the book. So what is an example of a bad decision?

Stuart: Mole didn't know how to row a boat, but he tried to row Rat's boat anyway. He crashed the boat, and nearly drowned. That was a very poor decision.

Claire: I bet Rat was in agony. He lost his boat.

Stuart: I never thought of it that way. What was the joy that everyone missed?

Wilma: The joy of being a child.

Jeremy: I think you are right. Everyone wanted Mr. Toad to grow up, and he just wanted to have fun. In the end, Mr. Toad remained childlike and happy, unlike Mouse. Grahame always hoped Mouse would grow up and become responsible. Unlike Mr. Toad, Mouse never had the chance.

Narrator Two: Kenneth Grahame gave us one of the most beloved books ever written. Next time you read *The Wind in the Willows,* think about the man who wrote books as his escape.

From *Multi-Grade Readers Theatre: Picture Book Authors and Illustrators* by Suzanne I. Barchers and Charla R. Pfeffinger. Santa Barbara, CA: Teacher Ideas Press/Libraries Unlimited. Copyright © 2009.

From Dolls to Designs

Kate Greenaway

1846–1901

Summary and Background Information

Kate Greenaway, renowned for her watercolors of dresses and gardens, was encouraged by her father to draw from the time she could hold a pencil. A master engraver, her father introduced her to people in the publishing field who could advance her career. Ms. Greenaway's first book was immensely popular, and she enjoyed several years of popularity. Her illustrations were so admired that they were often pirated. As her life entered its final years, her popularity declined. She struggled to maintain her lifestyle, dying at age fifty-four of breast cancer. The Kate Greenaway Medal, established in 1955, honors a distinguished artist living in Great Britain.

Presentation Suggestions

Kate Greenaway should stand in the middle with her family members on one side and her friends on the other side. The narrators can stand on either side of the staging area.

Introductory and Follow-up Suggestions

Display a variety of books that have won the Caldecott Medal and the Kate Greenaway Medal. Then ask:

- What do the stickers on these books stand for?

- Do you know how the two awards are different? (If the students don't know, explain that they'll learn the answer during the script.)

Show Great Britain on a map. Point out London. Explain that Kate Greenaway lived in Hoxton, which was near London in the 1800s. (It is now part of Greater London.) After reading the script ask:

- Kate Greenaway and Randolph Caldecott knew each other as adults. What distinguishes their awards? (The Caldecott Medal, established in 1937, is for distinguished American picture books; the Kate Greenaway medal is for distinguished illustrators from Great Britain.)

- If time allows, share the winner and the honor books from a few years. Ask the students to determine if they would have chosen those books as winners. Discuss what makes a picture book distinguished.

Characters

Grade Two: Elizabeth Greenaway, Edmund Evans

Grade Three: John Greenaway, Thomas Crane, Kate Greenaway, Randolph Caldecott

Grade Four: Narrator One, Narrator Two, Narrator Three

From Dolls to Designs

Narrator One: Born in 1846, Kate lives with her family in Hoxton, which is near London. She has a brother and two sisters. Her favorite family member is her father.

Narrator Two: Mr. John Greenaway is a fine engraver. Engraving is a way of making drawings on paper or metal. Mr. Greenaway gives Kate a pencil as soon as she can hold one.

John Greenaway: Hold the pencil like this, Kate. You can make your own illustrations on this paper and be an artist like me.

Elizabeth Greenaway: John, Kate doesn't want to draw pictures. She's too little and only wants to play with her dress-up dolls.

John Greenaway: Now, just look at her very first drawing, my dear. I think Kate is going to develop into a fine artist.

Elizabeth Greenaway: Well, that is a wonderful drawing. You might just be right about Kate. But we need to talk about what we are going to do about our income, John. With your mother and sisters to support, we need more money coming in. I'd like to open a dress shop. If we moved to Islington, I could make clothes for children.

John Greenaway: I hate to think of you working as a dressmaker, but times are hard. And you are very talented at it.

Elizabeth Greenaway: So it's settled, then. You start looking for a shop, and I'll start thinking about dress patterns.

Narrator Three: The dress shop is a success. Before long, Mrs. Greenaway has added lady's clothing and hats to her line. Kate spends many happy hours in the shop, watching the people. She notices all the latest fashions and never forgets them.

From *Multi-Grade Readers Theatre: Picture Book Authors and Illustrators* by Suzanne I. Barchers and Charla R. Pfeffinger. Santa Barbara, CA: Teacher Ideas Press/Libraries Unlimited. Copyright © 2009.

Narrator One: Kate goes to art school when she is twelve years old. Ten years later, her father helps Kate start her art career. She is just twenty-two years old when she has a small art exhibit. That leads to Kate doing some magazine illustrations. Thomas Crane, who works for a company that makes greeting cards, calendars, and books, also sees her work.

Thomas Crane: Miss, I'd like you to do some work for us. We need illustrations for our cards and calendars. Would you be interested?

Kate Greenaway: I'd like to do some illustrations for you. What kind of income might I expect from the drawings?

Thomas Crane: We would pay you three pounds for each illustration.

Kate Greenaway: All right, let's work out the arrangements.

Narrator Two: One of Kate's card designs sells 25,000 copies in a few weeks. The Marcus Ward Company does very well with her work. Yet they refuse to return the drawings to Kate when they are done with them. After six years, she quits working for them. Kate's father helps again.

John Greenaway: Kate, I want you to show your work to Edmund Evans. I think he'd consider your drawings for a book.

Kate Greenaway: I'm not sure about this idea, Father. But I suppose it won't hurt to show him some drawings.

Narrator Three: Kate shows her portfolio and poetry to Mr. Evans. He likes her drawings and has an idea.

Edmund Evans: Kate, I like your drawings. I'm sure you know that I do wood blocks for my printing. What do you think about that treatment for your art?

Kate Greenaway: What would I be illustrating? Will you use my poetry, too?

Edmund Evans: As a matter of fact, I do have an idea. I would like to bring out a book, but your poetry needs some work. I know a poet who could polish the poems. We'll bring out your book in color, and it should do very well indeed.

From *Multi-Grade Readers Theatre: Picture Book Authors and Illustrators* by Suzanne I. Barchers and Charla R. Pfeffinger. Westport, CT: Teacher Ideas Press/Libraries Unlimited. Copyright © 2009.

Narrator One: Mr. Evans is right. The book, called *Under the Window,* is a huge success. Kate is able to help the family move to a better neighborhood. Kate continues her interest in clothing. She spends happy hours designing the dresses that she then paints in her drawings. She plants flowers in her garden so that she can draw them.

Narrator Two: Mr. Evans helps her by introducing her to his friends.

Edmund Evans: Kate, I'd like you to meet my friend, Randolph Caldecott. He is an artist, too.

Randolph Caldecott: I'm happy to meet you, Miss Greenaway. But I wish you weren't quite so talented.

Kate Greenaway: What do you mean?

Randolph Caldecott: I'm afraid people will prefer your books to mine!

Kate Greenaway: Well, I hope you're right, but I think your work is wonderful. I doubt that you need to worry about my work.

Narrator Three: Kate and Randolph become friends, even though they are competing for book sales. Kate's books are very successful. People start using her art for things such as scarves, plates, and dolls. They don't have permission to use her work.

Kate Greenaway: Father, I'm going to change how I do things. I'm going to keep my original art, and I'll just sell the rights for using them.

John Greenaway: I don't think that will totally solve the problem, but it should help. I hope your work is always this popular!

Narrator One: Mr. Greenaway's words may have predicted the future. Kate enjoys many years of success. She buys an even nicer house. Then people seem to lose interest in her books. Sales begin to decline. Then, in 1890, her father dies. Four years later, her mother dies.

Narrator Two: Kate has to cut back on expenses. She does more paintings and portraits, hoping to raise money. In 1900, she learns that she has cancer, and a year later she dies. She is just fifty-four years old. Her work has not been lost, however. Millions of people have enjoyed her watercolors.

Narrator Three: In 1955, the Library Association of Great Britain establishes the Kate Greenaway Medal. This award honors the most distinguished illustrator living in Great Britain. Kate Greenaway will never be forgotten.

From *Multi-Grade Readers Theatre: Picture Book Authors and Illustrators* by Suzanne I. Barchers and Charla R. Pfeffinger. Santa Barbara, CA: Teacher Ideas Press/Libraries Unlimited. Copyright © 2009.

Once upon a Time . . .

Jacob Ludwig Carl Grimm

1785–1863

Wilhelm Carl Grimm

1786–1859

Summary and Background Information

Jacob and Wilhelm Grimm were born in Hanau, Germany, to Philipp Wilhelm Grimm, a lawyer and court official, and his wife Dorothea. Their parents had nine children; however, only six survived infancy. Their father's death led them to move from their pleasant country environs to a small urban house. The brothers studied law and eventually became librarians. Fascinated with folktales, they published *Children and Household Tales* in 1812, their first collection, which includes eighty-two folktales. They continued to gather folktales and publish several volumes, eventually becoming librarians and professors at the University of Göttingen. In this script, clues to titles of folktales collected by two famous writers (the Grimm Brothers) are provided through ten folktale guests. The identity of the writers is prompted at the end of the script. All of the students or the audience can respond to the prompts.

Presentation Suggestions

Guests 1 through 10 can sit in chairs. The narrators can stand on either side of the seated Guests.

Introductory and Follow-up Suggestions

Tell students that the name of this script is "Once upon a time." Then ask:

- What do you think of when you hear the words "Once upon a time"? What stories start that way?

- How old do you think these stories are?

If preferred, have the audience figure out the names of the writers upon the conclusion of the script. Then share the dates of their lives and find Germany on a map. Students can also vote on which story is their favorite. Discuss how these stories are similar to and different from Hans Christian Andersen's literary fairy tales.

Characters

Grade Two: Guest Four, Guest Five, Guest Six, Guest Seven

Grade Three: Guest One, Guest Two, Guest Three, Guest Nine, Guest Ten

Grade Four: Narrator One, Narrator Two, Guest Eight

Once upon a Time . . .

Narrator One: Once upon a time, long, long ago, there lived two men. They were librarians, and they loved stories.

Narrator Two: They loved stories so much that they collected them and wrote them down. In fact, they became two of the most famous writers in the world.

Narrator One: Let's see if you can figure out who these famous writers were. Our guests will give you a clue about the title of a story. You can say the title of the story. When we're done, you will probably be able to name the writers. Ready?

Students or Audience: Ready!

Guest One: I was kept in a tower by a witch, and I had really long hair.

Students or Audience: Rapunzel!

Guest Two: My brother and I visited a cottage in the woods. I saved him from being pushed into an oven.

Students or Audience: Hansel and Gretel!

Guest Three: I had to spend most of my time cooking and cleaning. Then a fairy godmother sent me to the ball where I met the prince.

Students or Audience: Cinderella!

Guest Four: I love wearing the color red. A mean wolf tricked my grandmother and me.

Students or Audience: Little Red Riding Hood!

Guest Five: All I ever wanted was to have a baby of my own. I never thought the queen would guess my name.

Students or Audience: Rumplestiltskin!

From *Multi-Grade Readers Theatre: Picture Book Authors and Illustrators* by Suzanne I. Barchers and Charla R. Pfeffinger. Santa Barbara, CA: Teacher Ideas Press/Libraries Unlimited. Copyright © 2009.

Narrator Two: Bravo! You have gotten the first five stories right. Now the next stories aren't as well known, so they are going to get a little bit harder. If you can't figure out the answer, our guest will give you another clue.

Guest Six: I had to save my brothers who had been turned into swans.

Narrator One: *(pausing)* Can you provide us with another clue?

Guest Six: There were six brothers.

Students or Audience: The Six Swans!

Guest Seven: I am one of a group of elves who helped a poor man.

Narrator Two: *(pausing)* A helpful group of elves is a good clue, but we seem to need a little help too.

Guest Seven: The man was a shoemaker. You should be able to put it all together now.

Students or Audience: The Elves and the Shoemaker!

Guest Eight: I am part of a group too, but we were poor animals. We went on a journey together and had an adventure.

Narrator One: *(pausing)* Can you tell us some more about what happened on this adventure?

Guest Eight: We came upon a house of robbers and decided to trick them. Those foolish men thought we were musicians!

Students or Audience: The Bremen Town Musicians!

Guest Nine: In this story, I scared away some robbers, too. But that was just one of many adventures.

Narrator Two: *(pausing)* It looks like we'll need some more information to figure out this one.

Guest Nine: Well, I'm not very big in this story. In fact, I'm no bigger than something you each have on your hand.

Students or Audience: Tom Thumb!

Guest Ten: I went from being a poor fisherman to being rich and then back to being poor.

From *Multi-Grade Readers Theatre: Picture Book Authors and Illustrators* by Suzanne I. Barchers and Charla R. Pfeffinger. Santa Barbara, CA: Teacher Ideas Press/Libraries Unlimited. Copyright © 2009.

Narrator One: *(pausing)* I think if you give another clue about how you got rich, we can get this one.

Guest Ten: I caught a fish that granted us three wishes, and my wife made poor choices.

Students or Audience: The Fisherman and His Wife!

Narrator Two: You've identified ten stories by these writers. We're going to take turns giving you a few more clues.

Narrator One: These two men lived more than two hundred years ago. There weren't a lot of books for children, so people told stories that they made up or heard.

Narrator Two: The two men listened to a lot of people tell stories and wrote them down.

Narrator One: Now listen carefully to these last two clues. Some stories had happy endings, and some were quite grim.

Narrator Two: And the last clue is that they were brothers. Just put it all together and you'll have the answer!

A Munster of a Writer

Fred Gwynne
1926–1993

Summary and Background Information

Fred Gwynne built a successful acting career long before he turned to writing books for children. With his talent for singing and acting, he was sought out for roles on Broadway. In 1961, he became familiar to television viewers for his role as Officer Francis Muldoon on *Car 54, Where Are You?* He won the role of Herman Munster on *The Munsters* because of his height and booming voice. In this script, the primary cast of *The Munsters* discusses their departure from the show and agrees to meet ten years later. They then discuss Fred Gwynne's first book, *The King Who Rained.* Although the information about the characters is real, the conversation is fictionalized.

Presentation Suggestions

The narrators should stand on either side of the other readers, who can be seated informally in chairs. If props are preferred, students can research the appearance of the set for *The Munsters* and add similar touches.

Introductory and Follow-up Suggestions

Write the names of some of the television shows from the 1960s on the board, such as *Bewitched, The Andy Griffith Show, Gilligan's Island,* or *The Dick Van Dyke Show.* Discuss which ones the students have watched. Then ask:

- Have you watched a television show called *The Munsters*? If the students are not familiar with the show, explain that it was about an oddball family of monsters, trying to live what they considered a rather normal life.

- Explain that the script is about the actors from *The Munsters* and that one also became a successful children's book writer.

After reading the script, read aloud one or more of Fred Gwynne's books. Then have the students create their own examples of wordplay using homophones or homonyms. An excellent source for finding examples of these is *The Reading Teacher's Book of Lists,* 5th edition, by Edward B. Fry and Jacqueline E. Kress (San Francisco: Jossey-Bass, 2006).

Characters

Grade Two: Al Lewis, Mel Blanc, Noel Blanc

Grade Three: Fred Gwynne, Butch Patrick, Pat Priest, Foxy Gwynne

Grade Four: Narrator One, Narrator Two, Yvonne DeCarlo

A Munster of a Writer

Narrator One: *The Munsters* was a TV show about a family of oddball monsters. The first show was in 1964. It lasted only two seasons. The actors talk about the end of the show.

Fred Gwynne: I sure hate to see this show end. However, I won't miss putting on that padding and having lifts in my boots.

Yvonne DeCarlo: I'll miss playing your wife, but I won't miss wearing all that makeup!

Al Lewis: I won't miss that makeup either. Mel, I think you had the easiest role of all. You just had to say "Nevermore."

Mel Blanc: That's true, but that one word could sure stir up Fred! Nevermore! Nevermore! Nevermore!

Fred Gwynne: Now stop teasing me, Mel! You know I'd never get mad at you. It was always my character Herman getting mad at that pesky raven.

Butch Patrick: I'll probably never have a role as good as this one. The best episodes were when we rode in the Munster Koach.

Pat Priest: I thought the Dragula was great, too. I wonder what we'll all be doing ten years from now? Let's agree that we'll get together then and see how we're all doing in our careers.

Fred Gwynne: Pat, that's a terrific idea. Do you mind organizing it for everyone? Maybe Mel will have learned a new word by then.

Mel Blanc: Just you wait! Well, I have to go. Bugs and the others are waiting for me. Th-th-th-that's all folks!

Narrator Two: Ten years later, the group gathers again. Fred has brought along his wife, Foxy. Mel greets everyone in one of his most famous voices.

Mel Blanc: What's up, Doc? Hey, everyone. Meet my son, Noel, and then tell us what you've been doing lately.

From *Multi-Grade Readers Theatre: Picture Book Authors and Illustrators* by Suzanne I. Barchers and Charla R. Pfeffinger. Santa Barbara, CA: Teacher Ideas Press/Libraries Unlimited. Copyright © 2009.

Fred Gwynne: Noel, it's great to see you and everyone else again. I brought along my wife, Foxy. She'll agree that I miss being Herman Munster a lot.

Foxy Gwynne: He may miss the show and working with all of you, but he's keeping pretty busy. He's got two careers going.

Al Lewis: I've seen you in a couple of Broadway shows, Fred. How would you have time for anything else?

Fred Gwynne: Well, you know I've always like to play around with words. And I studied art after I got out of the navy. So I came up with this little book idea, and a publisher liked it.

Foxy Gwynne: It's not just a little idea. It's a very clever idea.

Noel Blanc: This sounds mysterious. Is the book out yet? Have you brought a copy along?

Foxy Gwynne: I just happen to have a copy in my handbag. But I'll let Fred explain what it's about while you take a look at it.

Fred Gwynne: It's called *The King Who Rained.* It builds on the idea that some words sound the same. But these words are spelled differently. They also have different meanings. So, instead of a king reigning, or ruling, over his kingdom, this king is raining like he's a cloud.

Yvonne DeCarlo: That really *is* clever. I just thought of another example—rein, like the reins you hold when riding a horse. Aren't those called homophones?

Fred Gwynne: You're right. Not all of the book uses homophones, however. Some are things that would just make kids laugh. They are examples of misunderstandings that kids might have.

Butch Patrick: You mean like this page where the girl says that her daddy has a mole on his nose?

Noel Blanc: Look at that drawing, everyone. Who does it remind you of?

Everyone: Fred!

Noel Blanc: Here's a funny page. This one says that boars are coming to dinner. I can see how kids would get confused easily.

Mel Blanc: Are you going to do any other books, Fred?

Fred Gwynne: Well, they were pretty happy with this one. So my next one is coming out any day now.

Al Lewis: What's your next book called? *The King's Thrown*? You know, thrown like a ball, instead of the throne that a king sits on.

Fred Gwynne: Very funny, Al, but not a bad idea. This one is called *A Chocolate Moose for Dinner.* But enough about me. Time to hear what the rest of you are doing.

Narrator One: All of the Munster friends acted on Broadway, on TV, or in movies. For many years, Al wore his Munster suit as the host of horror movies on TV. Yvonne had a beautiful singing voice and performed in many Broadway shows. She also had roles in horror films.

Narrator Two: Mel Blanc did the voices for dozens of cartoon characters. He trained his son Noel to do voice characterization. Noel took over many of Mel's voices after Mel died.

Narrator One: Butch had many TV roles, played in a rock band, and has been co-host of *Macabre Theatre.* Pat was also on many TV shows, such as *Bewitched*, and in films.

Narrator Two: Fred kept acting until 1992, a year before he died. He also kept writing for children. His books with wordplay and jokes still make kids and adults laugh today.

Seeing the Magic

Trina Schart Hyman
1939–2004

Summary and Background Information

Trina Schart Hyman loved fairy tales, especially "Little Red Riding Hood." She knew from a young age that she wanted to be an artist. Although very bright, she was miserable in school until she attended art college in Philadelphia. She married young and moved with her husband for his work, studying art along the way. After her divorce, she worked for *Cricket* magazine during most of the 1970s. She struggled for many years to reconcile working with being a single mother. She has won many awards for her illustrations. She also gave frequent interviews and wrote about her experiences as an artist. This script was developed from her interviews and speeches.

Presentation Suggestions

Place the following readers in the back row: Narrator One, Narrator Two, Mother, Karleen, and Harris. Place the following readers in the front row: Librarian One, Librarian Two, Trina, Friend One, Friend Two. The stage can include artifacts from "Little Red Riding Hood," such as a red cape, basket of goodies, and a stuffed wolf or dog. When assigning roles, note that the last two readings by Trina are excerpted directly from her Caldecott acceptance speech. Therefore, the readability is higher than Grade Three and should be rehearsed by the reader.

Introductory and Follow-up Suggestions

Read aloud Trina Schart Hyman's *Little Red Riding Hood*. Explore the illustrations, especially the details in the borders. Then ask:

- Did you have a favorite story when you were a preschooler?

- Did you act it out? If so, what character were you?

- What is your favorite fairy tale now?

After reading the script, ask:

- What challenges did Trina Schart Hyman face in her life?
- What kind of art would you want to make if you could be an artist? Paintings? Watercolors? Black and white? Cut paper?

Discuss other illustrators' styles and contrast them with Trina Schart Hyman's.

Characters

Grade Two: Mother, Karleen

Grade Three: Trina, Harris, Librarian One, Librarian Two, Friend One, Friend Two

Grade Four: Narrator One, Narrator Two

Seeing the Magic

Narrator One: Trina listens to her mother read to her. She is finishing "Little Red Riding Hood."

Trina: Read it again, Mommy. You know that's my most favorite story.

Mother: I've read it three times today, Trina! That's enough. You can probably read it to yourself by now.

Narrator Two: Trina can read the story. She realized when she was four years old that the words on the page matched the words she was hearing. But she still loved hearing her mother and father read to her.

Mother: Besides, I have something for you, Trina. Look what I made for you.

Trina: It's a cape, just like Little Red Riding Hood's! Mommy, can I use that basket in the kitchen? Tippy can be the big bad wolf, and I can go to grandmother's house! Thank you, Mommy!

Mother: Your grandmother lives hundreds of miles away! Do you really think you can make it all that way? You need to get back before dinner.

Trina: Don't worry, Mommy. I'll be back as soon as the woodsman rescues grandmother and me!

Mother: Then let me put some goodies in that basket. Don't forget, Trina. *Don't speak to any strangers!*

Narrator One: Trina spends many happy hours playing in her backyard. Tippy doesn't even realize he's the wolf. When her father returns home each day, she greets him happily, just as if she is escaping a real wolf.

Narrator Two: Before long, it is time for Trina to attend school. She skips first grade, but she dislikes following all the rules. She prefers doodling and drawing pictures.

Narrator One: When she's at home, Trina loves to play with her younger sister, Karleen. They both enjoy stories, paper dolls, and fanciful games. The years pass, and Trina begins attending art school.

Karleen: What is college like, Trina?

Trina: It's wonderful at art college! I don't get in trouble for drawing all day. That's what they expect the students to do.

Karleen: What are the other students like?

Trina: They are all different, but they are also all the same. They are all artists, and we talk, eat, live, and dream about art.

Narrator Two: Trina gets married when she is in college. Her husband gets a job and they move around for his career. She studies art in Boston and Sweden. She learns about book design and printmaking. One day, while they are living in Sweden, she tells Harris, her husband, some news.

Trina: Harris, I've been asked to illustrate a book!

Harris: That's exciting news, Trina! What is the book about? What kind of illustrations will you draw?

Trina: It's a children's book, but I don't know what it is about yet. It's in Swedish, so I'll have to translate it before I can start.

Harris: How long will it take you to do the illustrations?

Trina: I've never illustrated a book before. I just don't know. First I have to figure out the story!

Narrator One: Trina's career has begun. She and Harris return to the United States. A few years after the birth of their daughter, they get a divorce. Trina is now a single mother, trying to raise Katrin and earn a living.

From *Multi-Grade Readers Theatre: Picture Book Authors and Illustrators* by Suzanne I. Barchers and Charla R. Pfeffinger. Westport, CT: Teacher Ideas Press/Libraries Unlimited. Copyright © 2009.

Narrator Two: Trina moves with some friends to New Hampshire. She goes to work for *Cricket* magazine. She directs the art program. *Cricket* becomes one of the best magazines for children. She does her own art, too. In 1984, her career gets a big boost when the phone rings early one January morning.

Librarian One: Good morning, Trina. I am with the Caldecott committee. Are you sitting down?

Trina: I'm sitting now!

Librarian One: Good news, Trina. You've won the Caldecott Honor Medal for *Little Red Riding Hood.*

Narrator One: This is a big honor, but a bigger honor comes a year later. The phone rings again one January morning.

Librarian Two: Trina, I hope you're awake. Great job again! This time you've won the Caldecott Medal for *Saint George and the Dragon.*

Narrator Two: Trina talks with some friends after she gets the call about the award.

Friend One: I am so excited for you, Trina. This is the highest honor you can get. Have you started thinking about what you'll say when you receive the award?

Trina: I have been thinking more about my art and my life. I would like to get out of the publishing business. I feel like I'm in a rut, but I need to make a living. I don't know how else to do that except with book illustrating.

Friend Two: That's the way it is for anyone trying to raise a child alone. You have to make difficult choices, but you don't have to get in a rut.

Trina: I wouldn't give up being an artist, and I wouldn't give up having a child. I do need to make a living, but I think I need to do some art just for myself. That might help bring some balance to my life—if I can find the time! I need to write that speech before I change my life!

Friend One: I know your speech will be just as great as your illustrations.

Narrator One: Trina does write a great speech. This portion talks about how she thinks about her drawings.

Trina: I think I was born drawing. I drew because I needed to as well as for the sheer joy of it. I feel like an actor preparing for a role when I'm working on a book. I need to get inside my characters and begin to think and feel their thoughts and feelings before I can succeed in my illustrations. . . .

Narrator Two: Trina's words conclude our story of a truly magical artist.

Trina: One of the nicest things about being an artist is the ability to see things a little differently, a little more carefully, perhaps a little more imaginatively, than most other people do. . . To be able to see the possibilities in things; to see the magic in them . . . .

From *Multi-Grade Readers Theatre: Picture Book Authors and Illustrators* by Suzanne I. Barchers and Charla R. Pfeffinger. Santa Barbara, CA: Teacher Ideas Press/Libraries Unlimited. Copyright © 2009.

A Frog and a Toad

Arnold Lobel

1933–1987

Summary and Background Information

Arnold Lobel used drawing and oral storytelling to fill his time as a child. He was often sick and missed a lot of school. When returning to school in the third grade, he was behind the rest of his classmates and was often picked on. His storytelling and drawings won over his classmates. An early illustrator for magazines and ads, he illustrated his first book, *Red Tag Come Back*, in 1961. The first book he wrote, *Mister Muster,* was the product of his many visits to the Prospect Park Zoo with his family. The Frog and Toad series came about as a request from an editor who was looking for something to catch the attention of children as a follow-up to Dr. Seuss and the books based on the Dolch word lists. Using creative watercolor sketches, repetition, and short sentences, Lobel was able to build a series of books on friendship with humor and events that children easily related to.

Presentation Suggestions

The narrator should sit to one side of the staging area. The other readers should sit on the opposite side of the staging area. The girls can stand behind a table to do their puppet show. The Toad and Frog puppets can be made quickly by gluing an oversized picture of a toad and a frog to a brown paper bag. A third bag can have the face of a man drawn on it to represent the author. If you are not using the puppet show props, the suggested actions in the script can be ignored.

Introductory and Follow-up Suggestions

Before reading the script, have the students list the differences between a frog and a toad. Then ask:

- Where do frogs live?

- Where do toads live?

> • How do most frogs and toads survive in the wintertime?

After reading the script, ask:

> • How many of Frog and Toad's characteristics are like real frogs and toads?

Characters

Grade Two: Tricia, Willis, Jeremy

Grade Three: Mr. Dayton, JoEllen, Corbin, Troy, Ada, Damon, Maria, Freddie

Grade Four: Narrator, Samantha

A Frog and a Toad

Narrator: Mr. Dayton has asked his class to do reports on a book or an author.

Samantha: Mr. Dayton, JoEllen, Tricia, and I all like the same series of books. May we work together on a report?

Mr. Dayton: That is a good idea. I expect it to be a special report if you work together.

JoEllen: We promise it will be really good.

Narrator: The day has finally come for the last group to do their report.

Mr. Dayton: Girls, it is time for your report.

Tricia: We need just a few minutes to set up our things. . . .

JoEllen: *(Male Puppet)* My name is Arnold Lobel. These are my two best friends, Frog and Toad.

Samantha: *(Frog Puppet)* We are his best friends because we made him very famous.

JoEllen: An editor asked me to write a book. The first book I wrote for him was called *Frog and Toad Are Friends*.

Samantha and Tricia: That's us!

Tricia: *(Toad Puppet)* We became a series of books. They are called easy readers.

JoEllen: I use very short sentences in my books.

Samantha: And he uses the same words over and over and over and over.

Tricia: We sound silly when we talk.

JoEllen: That may be, but children quickly learn how to read.

Tricia: Our books have very short chapters in them.

From *Multi-Grade Readers Theatre: Picture Book Authors and Illustrators* by Suzanne I. Barchers and Charla R. Pfeffinger. Santa Barbara, CA: Teacher Ideas Press/Libraries Unlimited. Copyright © 2009.

Samantha: Our books aren't just about words and chapters. They are about a loving friendship between Toad and Frog.

JoEllen: The books are funny, too. And it is easy to guess what will happen next in my stories. Each of you is a unique character in my stories.

Samantha: I am always very calm. I love to be outdoors and do things.

Tricia: I get very excited. I shout a lot. I grumble, too. And I am always worrying.

Samantha: It is up to me to help Toad when he gets upset. I especially need to help him when he tries to be brave.

Tricia: I can't help the way I am. I didn't write me this way!

JoEllen: I made each of you very different. You balance each other out. Where Toad is weak, Frog is strong. When one of you is funny, the other is serious. Regardless of what you two go through, you are always good friends.

Samantha: I am a great storyteller. Does anyone know the titles of the books where I tell good stories?

Willis: In *Days with Frog and Toad* you told the story "Shivers."

Corbin: You told the story "The Corner" in *Frog and Toad All Year.* I really like that story.

Tricia: I wish I could have told a story.

JoEllen: Toad, you are not a storyteller. Your purpose is to make readers feel good. You even make readers laugh.

Tricia: Is that a good thing?

Samantha: Yes it is. Everyone needs a good laugh.

Tricia: Let's see if you are right. Who can tell me something I did that made them laugh?

Troy: You planted a garden. You kept shouting at the seed to make them grow. Then you started to worry that you have scared them and they won't grow. Next you start to sing and dance!

From *Multi-Grade Readers Theatre: Picture Book Authors and Illustrators* by Suzanne I. Barchers and Charla R. Pfeffinger. Santa Barbara, CA: Teacher Ideas Press/Libraries Unlimited. Copyright © 2009.

Ada: I thought it was funny when you went to buy Frog an ice cream cone. You bought two of them and they melted before you ever got to give one to Frog. You were a huge chocolate mess!

JoEllen: Now don't you feel better about yourself, Toad? You have made people laugh. I made you look different, also.

Tricia: Was that supposed to make people laugh, too? I am short and fat and brown. Frog is tall, green and is a snappy dresser. Could I have a better wardrobe?

Samantha: You don't need a new wardrobe to be a good friend or to make me feel better. Remember when I was sick and you came to take care of me? That is more important than how you look or dress.

JoEllen: Very well said, Frog. Does anyone have any questions about my books or me?

Damon: Who does the illustrations for your books?

JoEllen: I do all of them. Which ones do you like the best?

Damon: The fear you drew on their faces when the rocks were falling toward them. That was in the book *Dragons and Giants.*

Troy: I liked the sketches of Toad while he waited for his seeds to grow.

Corbin: I liked the sketches of the old dark frog in the story "Shivers" that Frog tells Toad. He was really scary.

Willis: Did you only write books about Frog and Toad?

JoEllen: I wrote *Mouse Soup* and *Grasshopper on the Road.* I wrote a lot of animal books.

Maria: Where do you get your models for the animals in your books?

JoEllen: A zoo was close to my apartment. I would go there often with my family. I could sketch the animals there.

Freddie: Where did the models for Frog and Toad come from?

From *Multi-Grade Readers Theatre: Picture Book Authors and Illustrators* by Suzanne I. Barchers and Charla R. Pfeffinger. Santa Barbara, CA: Teacher Ideas Press/Libraries Unlimited. Copyright © 2009.

JoEllen: We went to Vermont a lot. There were toads and frogs all over Vermont.

Maria: Did you write or did you illustrate books first?

JoEllen: I did illustrations for other authors first. I was sick when I was in grade school. I missed all of second grade. While I was sick, I did a lot of drawing. I also told stories about my drawings, but I didn't write them down.

Jeremy: Where do your book ideas come from?

JoEllen: I am a daydreamer. I see the pictures in my mind. Then I come up with the words for the story I have drawn.

Jeremy: Did you ever want to do something else? Maybe be a doctor?

JoEllen: Never! Making books is too much fun.

Corbin: What do you use to make your drawings?

JoEllen: I always use watercolors. I like them best. I can fade one color into another with them. I think our time is up, isn't it Mr. Dayton?

Mr. Dayton: It was up a long time ago. But your puppet show was so interesting I hated to stop you. Thank you for all the work you did on your report, girls. Say goodbye!

Everyone: Goodbye!

Who Is the True Mother Goose?

Mother Goose aka Elizabeth Goose

1665–1758

Summary and Background Information

Some historians assert that the source for the Mother Goose rhymes was Elizabeth Goose, wife of Isaac Goose of Boston, Massachusetts. Elizabeth Foster married him when she was twenty-seven, raising his ten children, plus the six that they had together. There is no definitive answer to the question regarding the true origin of Mother Goose. Further, historians continue to speculate on the origins of many nursery rhymes. This script provides an introduction to the background of some popular nursery rhymes. The information has been gathered from *The Oxford Dictionary of Nursery Rhymes* edited by Iona and Peter Opie (New York, Oxford University Press, 1997). The punctuation for the rhymes, which are read by all the characters (Everyone), has been adapted to allow for easier reading.

Presentation Suggestions

Mother Goose can sit on a stool in the center of the stage with the nursery rhyme characters sitting at her feet. If preferred, the narrators can prompt the audience to join in with the reading of the rhymes by displaying chart paper or posters with the scripts. Additional readers can be assigned to the "Everyone" speakers.

Introductory and Follow-up Suggestions

Begin by reciting a few nursery rhymes, such as "Pat-a-cake," Pease Porridge Hot," or "Peter Peter Pumpkin-Eater." Then ask:

- What are your favorite nursery rhymes?

- How did you learn them?

- Where do you think they come from?

After reading the script, see how many more nursery rhymes the students can remember. Are there cultural differences in the students' nursery rhymes? If so, explore how they are alike and different.

Characters

Grade Two: Mother Goose, King of France, Georgie Porgie

Grade Three: Little Boy Blue, Old King Cole, Little Dog Gone, Mouse, Cat, Jack Horner, Jack be Nimble

Grade Four: Narrator One, Narrator Two, Little Bo-peep, Fly

Various Grades: Everyone

Who Is the True Mother Goose?

Narrator One: Have you ever wondered who the real Mother Goose is? Many people think she was Mrs. Elizabeth Goose. She lived in Boston in the late 1600s. She married a man who had ten children and then they had six more children. That is a lot of children to entertain!

Narrator Two: Some people believe that Mrs. Goose made up all the nursery rhymes, but that's not true. Nursery rhymes came from many different times and places. Just listen.

Mother Goose: It is true that I loved singing to my children. My daughter Elizabeth loved the rhymes, too. When she grew up, she married Thomas Fleet. He was a printer, and he wrote down many of the rhymes. I'm sorry to say that no one can find proof of that first book.

Little Bo-peep: I probably wasn't in that book. It was in a book printed in London in about 1777. Do you remember the rhyme?

Everyone: Little Bo-peep has lost her sheep, and can't tell where to find them. Leave them alone, and they'll come home, and bring their tails behind them.

Little Boy Blue: My rhyme is much older. Some people think that I am about Cardinal Wolsey. He was an advisor to King Henry the Eighth. That was in the early 1500s. Cardinal Wolsey had a lot of power. Here's my rhyme.

Everyone: Little Boy Blue, come blow your horn. The sheep's in the meadow. The cow's in the corn. Where is the boy who looks after the sheep? He's under the haystack, fast asleep. Will you wake him? No, not I. For if I do, he's sure to cry.

Mother Goose: Speaking of kings, we have a famous king here.

Old King Cole: Many people have tried to figure out where my song came from. Someone thought I was named after someone who lived in the third century. Now that is a very long time ago! Another person thought I was meant to be a rich clothing merchant who lived like a king. I like it that there is a bit of mystery about me, so I'm not going to tell the truth. Make an old man happy though. Read my song.

Everyone: Old King Cole was a merry old soul, and a merry old soul was he. He called for his pipe, and he called for his bowl, and called for his fiddlers three. Every fiddler he had a fiddle, and a very fine fiddle had he. Twee tweedle dee, tweedle dee, went the fiddlers. Oh, there's none so rare as can compare with King Cole and his fiddlers three.

King of France: Don't forget about me! You may not remember my verse, so let's say it now.

Everyone: The king of France went up the hill with forty thousand men. The king of France came down the hill and never went up again.

King of France: My verse is short. But I can tell you about it. I am King Henry the Fourth. I had a huge army in 1610. Sadly, I was killed soon after that march.

Georgie Porgie: Well, at least you know about your background. No one knows for sure about me. I like to think it's true that I was really Charles II. He was king of England in the 1600s. I guess I'll never know. But I still love to kiss girls—and run away!

Everyone: Georgie Porgie, pudding and pie. Kissed the girls and made them cry. When the boys came out to play, Georgie Porgie ran away.

Little Dog Gone: Most people don't know who wrote my song, but I do. Septimus Winner lived in Philadelphia in the late 1800s. He wrote music and published more than two thousand pieces. The song we sing is changed a little from what he wrote. But it's still my favorite song.

Everyone: Oh where, oh where has my little dog gone? Oh where, oh where can he be? With his ears cut short and his tail cut long, oh where, oh where is he?

Mother Goose: There are lots of other rhymes about animals. Let's hear from that mouse who loved to run up and down the clock.

Mouse: Don't you love the rhythm in my nursery rhyme? Hickory dickory dock. The mouse ran up the clock. Here's the truth about my rhyme. I come from Scotland, and shepherds used the rhyme to help count their sheep. Children would say the rhyme to decide who went first in a game. I've probably been around for hundreds of year, but I'm not too old to make that trip up the clock again.

Everyone: Hickory, dickory dock. The mouse ran up the clock. The clock struck one. The mouse ran down. Hickory, dickory, dock.

Cat: You're lucky I was busy with my fiddle or you might have been my lunch! My rhyme is called a nonsense verse. The first time I was written down was in 1765. There are all kinds of ideas about the meaning of my rhyme. No one knows for sure, but I don't think that matters. It's more important that it's fun.

Everyone: Hey diddle diddle. The cat and the fiddle. The cow jumped over the moon. The little dog laughed to see such sport. And the dish ran away with the spoon.

Fly: Speaking of fiddles, people were saying my rhyme at the same time. Back then, it started out like this. "Fiddle-dee-dee! Fiddle-dee-dee! The fly shall marry the humble-bee." I bet you never heard of a humble-bee before. It's just an old-fashioned way to say bumblebee. Let's say it the modern way.

Everyone: Fiddle-dee-dee! Fiddle-dee-dee! The fly shall marry the bumblebee. The bumblebee was never so glad as when she had met with so pretty a lad, as . . . Fiddle-dee-dee! Fiddle-dee-dee! The fly shall marry the bumblebee.

From *Multi-Grade Readers Theatre: Picture Book Authors and Illustrators* by Suzanne I. Barchers and Charla R. Pfeffinger. Westport, CT: Teacher Ideas Press/Libraries Unlimited. Copyright © 2009.

Mother Goose: Before we run out of time, let's hear from some of the men who share the same name—Jack. Little Jack Horner, would you like to start?

Jack Horner: This may be my story—or it may not be. I worked for an abbot when Henry the Eighth was king of England. The abbot sent me to London with a Christmas gift. It was a pie that had some important papers in it. I took those papers, and that gave me the right to own a manor, a very fine home. Of course my family thinks I bought the manor myself. A manor would be quite a "plum," but do you really think I'd steal from the king?

Everyone: Little Jack Horner sat in a corner, eating a Christmas pie. He put in his thumb and pulled out a plum. And said, "What a good boy am I!"

Jack be Nimble: My rhyme was just for fun. People in England liked to jump over a candlestick for luck. If you could jump over a candle without putting it out you'd have good luck in the next year. I guess if your skirt or pants caught on fire, you had bad luck right away!

Everyone: Jack be nimble. Jack be quick. Jack jump over the candlestick.

Mother Goose: I'm going to end with one last nursery rhyme. You may not have heard it before. This rhyme was told when children would keep asking for another story. Here it is: I'll tell you a story about Jack a Nory. And now my story's begun. I'll tell you another of Jack and his brother. And now my story is done!

Everyone: Goodbye!

From *Multi-Grade Readers Theatre: Picture Book Authors and Illustrators* by Suzanne I. Barchers and Charla R. Pfeffinger. Santa Barbara, CA: Teacher Ideas Press/Libraries Unlimited. Copyright © 2009.

Celebrating the Artist of Olvera Street

Leo Politi

1908–1996

Summary and Background Information

Leo Politi captured the heart of Los Angeles and its people in his children's books and countless artworks. He was called the "Artist of Olvera Street." Born in California, his parents moved the family to Italy in 1941 when World War II began. He returned to California in 1951 and established himself as an artist. Many of his watercolor illustrations were reproduced in *Bunker Hill,* written for the adult audience. The book chronicled the demolition of Bunker Hill in favor of large office buildings. He was referred to by many as a humorous man. Like many artists during those early years, he struggled financially, often selling his paintings for just enough money to put food on the dinner table. This script touches on the centennial celebration that took place during 2008 in the Los Angeles area. The Web site www.leopoliti2008centennial.org provides information about Mr. Politi and the celebration in his honor.

Presentation Suggestions

The narrators, Mrs. Flowers, and Mr. Garcia can sit on one side. Mr. Diaz should sit in the middle. The children should sit on the other side of the staging area. Books by Leo Politi can be displayed on the stage.

Introductory and Follow-up Suggestions

Start the group by discussing their birth year(s). Then ask:

- What is a centennial? What does it celebrate? Then share that people celebrated Leo Politi, a fine illustrator, during his centennial in 2008. Then ask in what year he would have been born.

- What is a migration of swallows? (Each year the swallows migrate back to the Mission San Juan Capistrano, on March 19, St. Joseph's Day.)

- Why would the swallows return to the same place year after year?

- What is a mission?

After the reading of the script, read aloud *The Song of the Swallows.* Invite students to do research on the migration of the swallows or missions.

Characters

Grade Two: Mrs. Flowers, Mr. Garcia, Felix

Grade Three: Susannah, Timothy, Hailey, Alanzo, Clarissa, Tito, Sara

Grade Four: Narrator One, Mr. Diaz, Narrator Two

Celebrating the Artist of Olvera Street

Narrator One: Mr. Diaz is meeting with Mrs. Flowers and Mr. Garcia. They run the summer reading clubs. He has an idea for finishing the coming summer program.

Mr. Diaz: How many children come to your summer reading clubs?

Mrs. Flowers: Last summer there were one hundred children who started the club. Only half read all of the books on their list. I think they get bored before they are done.

Mr. Diaz: I have an idea that may keep the kids reading throughout the program. The city is having a party. It's in honor of Leo Politi. All year long there will be events in his honor.

Mr. Garcia: We've heard about the events, and we have plans to honor him. His books will be on our reading lists.

Mr. Diaz: That provides the perfect start for my idea. I want to organize a Leo Politi Day. The children will have to finish all of their readings for the summer.

Mr. Garcia: What will the children do that day?

Mr. Diaz: First, they will go to a gallery to see Leo Politi's art. They will ride down Olvera Street and through Bunker Hill. We will go to lunch and then go to the San Juan Capistrano Mission. The kids will hear the story *Song of the Swallows*.

Mrs. Flowers: That sounds like a wonderful day! You know, you could have every child go on the trip who reads the books.

Mr. Diaz: Would either of you like to do the narration on the trip?

Mr. Garcia: I'd like to share that with you, Mrs. Flowers. We can learn more about Mr. Politi together.

Narrator Two: Just as they start to leave, they notice some children listening.

Susannah: Excuse me. Who is Mr. Politi?

Mr. Diaz: He is an author and artist who lived in Bunker Hill. He would take his easel to Olvera Street to make drawings of the children at play. He wrote books about the children who played in the neighborhood.

Timothy: Did you say the city is having a party for him? Why?

Mr. Diaz: If he were still alive, he would be one hundred years old this year. Everywhere you go there will be events in his honor.

Mrs. Flowers: Perhaps you can join the summer reading program. Then you can learn more.

Susannah: I'll ask my mother about signing up.

Timothy: Me too. She's checking out some library books now.

Narrator One: Soon, the summer reading clubs have come to an end. The children line up for the buses to take them on their trip in honor of Leo Politi.

Mr. Garcia: Boys and girls, this is Mr. Diaz. He organized the trip today.

Mr. Diaz: I hope every one of you enjoys the day.

Hailey: Mr. Diaz, are you going to go with us on our trip today?

Mr. Diaz: Unfortunately, I have some meetings at the library. I'll meet you at lunch and you can tell me all about your morning. I'll spend the afternoon with you at the mission.

Alanzo: Why are we visiting a mission, Mr. Diaz?

Mr. Diaz: I think I'll let you discover why this mission is special.

Narrator Two: The morning went very fast. When the children meet Mr. Diaz at lunch, they are all excited about what they have seen.

Felix: Mr. Diaz, did you know an artist lived right here in our city?

Mr. Diaz: Yes, I did, Felix. What did you learn about Leo Politi?

Clarissa: When he was six years old, he moved to Italy. His parents were from Italy.

Tito: In Italy he went to art school at age fifteen. He came back here when he was twenty-three years old.

Sara: We saw a lot of his paintings at the gallery. He liked to draw people and drew a lot of pictures of his wife, too. He liked to paint with watercolors. But it is sad, because no one paid him very much for his paintings. Now they are worth a lot of money.

Hailey: He did sculptures, and he wrote more than twenty books!

Mr. Diaz: Have any of you read any of his books?

Alanzo: I read some of his books, including one about a mission and swallows. Are we going to that mission?

Mr. Diaz: Yes, we are, Alanzo. While we are at the mission, we are going to hear the story that he wrote about the mission called *Song of the Swallows*. Is everyone done with lunch and ready to go? Then let's get on the buses.

Narrator One: At the mission, they hear Mr. Politi's story about Juan and the swallows. Swallows fly all around them.

Clarissa: Mr. Diaz, a swallow is sitting on your head!

Mr. Diaz: Swallows are very gentle birds. I am sure Juan didn't mind if they sat on his head either. Have you enjoyed your day?

Tito: It is the best day I have had in my whole life! I had never been to a gallery before. And I have never seen so many paintings before.

Sara: It was a wonderful day, Mr. Diaz. Thank you for | arranging this.

Mr. Diaz: Before we go, come with me to the front of the mission. I have a photographer waiting for us. Each one of you is going to get a copy of our photograph so you will always remember this day.

Felix: Will you stand beside me, Mr. Diaz? That way when I look at the picture I will always be able to find you in the picture.

Narrator Two: There were events to honor Mr. Politi for a full year in the Los Angeles area. You can see his paintings in the galleries and libraries in Los Angeles. If you can't get to Los Angeles, you can see his work on the Internet.

Narrator One: And if you can't get on the Internet, just go to your nearest library. You'll find wonderful books by Leo Politi. Check it out!

From *Multi-Grade Readers Theatre: Picture Book Authors and Illustrators* by Suzanne I. Barchers and Charla R. Pfeffinger. Santa Barbara, CA: Teacher Ideas Press/Libraries Unlimited. Copyright © 2009.

Tickle Me with Poetry

Shel Silverstein

1930–1999

Summary and Background Information

Shel Silverstein was a private man who granted few interviews. He loved drawing and writing as a child and built his career as a cartoonist when serving in the U.S. Army in Korea and Japan. He began writing for children with *ÿ* published in 1963. His fame grew with *The Giving Tree* in 1964, which met with both critical acclaim and criticism from feminists. Perhaps his most famous song was "A Boy Named Sue" recorded by Johnny Cash in 1969. With the publication of *Where the Sidewalk Ends* in 1974, he became a favorite of many children, parents, librarians, and teachers. This script provides an outline of his life, interspersed with poems from *Where the Sidewalk Ends, A Light in the Attic,* and *Falling Up.* The poems can be read by individual readers, in pairs, or as choral reading. Preread all poems for suitability for your students, substituting or skipping poems as preferred. The reading levels of the poems vary, so allow students to preview and practice them.

Presentation Suggestions

The narrator and students can sit in two or three rows, with Shel Silverstein sitting on a high stool in the center. Photocopies of the poems can be affixed to heavy stock paper so that students can follow the script and turn to their individual poems at the appropriate time. Alternatively, copy the poems onto a flip chart and turn to each poem as the presentation progresses. This has the added advantage of allowing a student to look up and toward the audience.

Introductory and Follow-up Suggestions

Show students copies of *Where the Sidewalk Ends, A Light in the Attic,* and *Falling Up.* Then ask:

- What is your favorite Shel Silverstein poem?

- What is your favorite Shel Silverstein book?

- What do you think he was like as a child?

Explain that this script will combine some information about his life with some of his poems. After reading the script and poems, ask:

- Can you think of other poems that fit with Shel Silverstein's life?

- What other poets do you enjoy reading?

Share collections of poetry by writers such as Jeff Moss, Jack Prelutsky, Aileen Fisher, and Bruce Lansky. Discuss how they are alike and different from Shel Silverstein.

Characters

Grade One: Reader Four, Reader Six, Reader Eight

Grade Two: Reader One, Reader Three, Reader Seven, Reader Twelve

Grade Three: Narrator, Shel Silverstein, Reader Eleven, Reader Thirteen, Reader Fourteen

Grade Four: Reader Two, Reader Five, Reader Nine, Reader Sixteen

Grade Five: Reader Ten, Reader Fifteen

Tickle Me with Poetry

Reader One: Reads "Where the Sidewalk Ends" from *Where the Sidewalk Ends*, p. 64.

Narrator: Shel Silverstein was born in Chicago in 1930. He died in Key West, Florida, in 1999. If Shel Silverstein were alive, this is what he—and his poems—might tell us.

Shelverstein: I was born in Chicago in 1930. When I was a teen, I wanted to be a baseball player. But I couldn't play baseball. I also wanted to be a hit with girls. But I couldn't even dance. It seemed like some kids, especially the girls, were hard to please.

Reader Two: Reads "Hard to Please" from *Falling Up*, p. 174.

Reader Three: Reads: "Whatif" from *A Light in the Attic*, p. 90.

Shelverstein: I started to draw cartoons and write poetry. I didn't know much about either, but I liked to think that I was clever.

Reader Four: Reads "Tell Me" from *Falling Up*, p. 154.

Shelverstein: I went into the army in the 1950s. I got to draw cartoons for a newspaper called *Stars and Stripes*. Sometimes I had too much fun with those cartoons. I would make fun of things in the military. I got into a bit of trouble. But not too much.

Reader Five: Reads "Somebody Has To" from *A Light in the Attic*, p. 28.

Shelverstein: I started writing children's books in the 1960s. It took a while for my books to sell well, so I wrote songs, too.

Reader Six: Reads "Boa Constrictor" from *Where the Sidewalk Ends*, p. 45.

Reader Seven: Reads "Rock 'n' Roll Band" from *A Light in the Attic*, p. 24

Shelverstein: I loved writing for kids and a book of poems called *Where the Sidewalk Ends* came out in 1974. I hoped I could make kids laugh.

Reader Eight: Reads "Ickle Me, Pickle Me, Tickle Me Too" from *Where the Sidewalk Ends*, p. 16.

Shelverstein: Some people think that my poems teach lessons to kids.

Reader Nine: Reads "It's Dark in Here" from *Where the Sidewalk Ends*, p. 21.

Reader Ten: Reads "Ladies First" from *A Light in the Attic*, p. 148.

Shelverstein: Some people think that they teach lessons to adults.

Reader Eleven: Reads "Obedient" from *Falling Up*, p. 90.

Reader Twelve: Reads "Ma and God" from *Where the Sidewalk Ends*, p. 119.

Shelverstein: Some people think my poems are rather weird.

Reader Thirteen: Reads "Reachin' Richard" from *Falling Up*, p. 93.

Shelverstein: Mostly I like to play with words.

Reader Fourteen: Reads "Shanna in the Sauna" from *Falling Up*, p. 104.

Shelverstein: You might also say that I like to turn things upside down. Or downside up.

Reader Fifteen: Reads "Reflection" from *A Light in the Attic*, p. 29.

Shelverstein: I'll read the next poem, which is exactly what I hope for all of you. Reads "Put Something In" from *A Light in the Attic*, p. 22.

Narrator: This last poem reminds us of all Shel Silverstein has given us.

Reader Sixteen: Reads "This Bridge" from *A Light in the Attic*, p. 169.

From Siberia to America

Esphyr Slobodkina
1908–2002

Summary and Background Information

Esphyr Slobodkina was born in Chelyabinsk, Siberia. The family moved to Ufa, Russia, in 1915, which began a series of moves prompted by the civil unrest in Russia. Esphyr and her family eventually moved to the United States, where she continued her art studies. After a brief marriage, she began illustrating children's books, thanks to an introduction to Margaret Wise Brown. She illustrated several of Ms. Brown's books, including *The Little Farmer, The Little Cowboy,* and so forth. The most enduring by Ms. Slobodkina is *Caps for Sale.*

Presentation Suggestions

Arrange readers in the following order: Narrator One through Narrator Three, Father, Mother, Ronya, Tamara, Esphyr, Ilya, Friend, and Margaret Wise Brown.

Introductory and Follow-up Suggestions

This script includes a variety of place names that may prove difficult for students to read. Write the following words on the board and discuss their pronunciations: Esphyr, Ufa, Siberia, Omsk, Vladivostok, Palestine, Harbin, Manchuria. Next, look up the following places on a map: Siberia, Ufa, Omsk, Vladivostok, Palestine, and Harbin, Manchuria. Then ask:

- How many of you have moved? More than once? Twice?

- What does it feel like to move?

Discuss the challenges of moving long distances, especially if you don't know the language in your new home. Explain that this story is about an author and illustrator who traveled thousands of miles to escape problems the government was having in the beginning of the twentieth century. After reading the script, ask:

- What characteristics do you think Esphyr and her family showed? (Courage, adaptability, determination, and the like)

- If you had to move, where would you like to live?

Read aloud *Caps for Sale,* which lends itself well to acting out.

Characters

Grade Two: Esphyr, Tamara, Margaret

Grade Three: Father, Mother, Ronya, Ilya, Friend

Grade Four: Narrator One, Narrator Two, Narrator Three

From Siberia to America

Narrator One: Esphyr and her family like living in Ufa, Russia. They have a bigger apartment than in Siberia, where Esphyr was born. Her father has a good job. Her mother is a talented singer. They have parties and go on sleigh rides. Then things begin to change in 1917. The Russian Civil War breaks out.

Narrator Two: Esphyr's favorite uncle is drafted into the White Army. He is killed in his first battle. Some of their friends are arrested. By 1918, Esphyr's father knows he must make a change.

Father: I am sending Mother and you girls to see Aunt Sonia. It should be safer there.

Esphyr: But she lives so far away. How will we get there?

Father: I've arranged passage on an oil tanker.

Tamara: An oil tanker? Eww! We'll probably starve to death.

Mother: I think you'll be pleasantly surprised. We'll eat with the captain and his wife. You'll get to go on several rivers—even the Volga River!

Esphyr: Well, it might be all right. But I'll be glad when we get to Aunt Sonia's house, have some real food, and see Grandmother.

Tamara: What about Ronya? Is he coming, too?

Father: No, he will stay behind. Think of this as a holiday for special young ladies.

Narrator Three: As promised, Esphyr and Tamara enjoy the journey. They also have fun visiting their relatives. The return journey is not as much fun. The war has made it hard to travel.

From *Multi-Grade Readers Theatre: Picture Book Authors and Illustrators* by Suzanne I. Barchers and Charla R. Pfeffinger. Westport, CT: Teacher Ideas Press/Libraries Unlimited. Copyright © 2009.

Narrator One: When they finally arrive home, they have to share their apartment with relatives who are homeless. They fear there will be food shortages. Then they learn that Grandmother has died. The family decides they must leave again.

Mother: Children, we are leaving, this time for good. We are selling everything we can. We'll give away the rest.

Esphyr: Where are we going?

Father: First we are going to go on a troop train. We'll stop to visit an uncle, and then we'll get to Omsk. We'll take the Trans-Siberian Express train from there.

Ronya: Trains! I'm going to pack all my suitcases!

Father: Only one suitcase each—and you have to carry it. Once we get to Vladivostok, we'll try to get a ship to Palestine.

Ronya: We're also going on a ship? What an adventure!

Narrator Two: It is an adventure, but a shortened one. They are unable to find a ship, so they have to find a place to live in Vladivostok. They find a small house and for three years watch their fortune slip away. Something has to change, so Mother and Father make another decision.

Mother: Girls, you and I are going to Harbin in Manchuria, where I am going to work as a dressmaker.

Ronya: What about Father and me?

Father: It looks like I'll have a job soon, so you can stay with me and finish school.

Narrator Three: Mother builds a good business. The girls go to school and take art lessons. Ronya finishes high school and decides to go to America.

Narrator One: The Roaring Twenties have come to the United States. Esphyr loves the short dresses and new hairstyles. She has become a good dressmaker and enjoys a good life. But she dreams of going to America. The family talks about their future.

 From *Multi-Grade Readers Theatre: Picture Book Authors and Illustrators* by Suzanne I. Barchers and Charla R. Pfeffinger. Santa Barbara, CA: Teacher Ideas Press/Libraries Unlimited. Copyright © 2009.

Mother: The only way Esphyr can go to America is as a student. So she will go first and start school.

Tamara: Will Esphyr be going alone or will I be with her?

Father: Mother will go next and start working. Tamara, you'll join the family next, and I'll come last.

Narrator Two: Esphyr makes the long journey to New York City. Then she discovers that her brother has enrolled her in the wrong school. It is a missionary school. But she studies English there and goes to a design school in the evening until she can go to art school. Her mother finally arrives in 1929. Then they face more tough times.

Mother: Esphyr and Ronya, it is hard to find a good job. The country seems to be in a depression. I am going to open my own dressmaking salon. There are still wealthy women who want fine dresses.

Narrator Three: Tamara joins the family, and the girls go to art classes. Father joins the family in 1931. Esphyr becomes close with one student, a fine painter. Ilya visits her each week at home.

Ilya: Esphyr, please quit that art school and marry me. I know more than all your teachers put together.

Esphyr: Ilya, you keep proposing, but I'm just not sure it's right.

Ilya: Of course it's right. Besides, if we marry, you could become a citizen.

Narrator One: Esphyr finally gives in and marries Ilya, but it lasts only three years. They remain friends for many years. Meanwhile, another friend changes her life.

Friend: Esphyr, I think you should illustrate children's books. I want you to meet a writer friend of mine named Margaret Wise Brown.

Esphyr: That's a good idea. But I don't have any art like that to show someone. I'll need some time to get ready.

Narrator Two: Ephyr creates some collages and takes them to show Margaret Wise Brown.

From *Multi-Grade Readers Theatre: Picture Book Authors and Illustrators* by Suzanne I. Barchers and Charla R. Pfeffinger. Santa Barbara, CA: Teacher Ideas Press/Libraries Unlimited. Copyright © 2009.

Margaret: I like your art, Esphyr. It's simple and honest. Let's talk about what we could do together.

Narrator Three: Esphyr illustrates several books written by Margaret Wise Brown. She works at a job to pay her bills. And she continues with her illustrations. She becomes well known for her many different works of art. But her true work of art for children is a book many of you probably know.

Narrator One: It starts like this: "Once there was a peddler who sold caps." Do you remember it?

Narrator Two: If you do, you probably know what the peddler said. If so, say it with me, "Caps. Caps for sale. Fifty cents a cap!"

Narrator Three: And if you don't know that story, it's time to check it out!

From *Multi-Grade Readers Theatre: Picture Book Authors and Illustrators* by Suzanne I. Barchers and Charla R. Pfeffinger. Santa Barbara, CA: Teacher Ideas Press/Libraries Unlimited. Copyright © 2009.

A Simple Life

Tasha Tudor

1915–2008

Summary and Background Information

Tasha Tudor had an unconventional upbringing for the times. Her mother retained her maiden name; her parents divorced when Tasha was nine years old; and she was raised by a family friend, "Aunt" Gwen, when her mother moved to Greenwich Village to pursue her painting. Although she enjoyed her time with her parents, her time with "Aunt" Gwen inspired a lifelong love of farming and living a simpler life. After her marriage, she began illustrating to help provide the funds for the purchase of a farm. She had four children and preferred to farm in the style of the 1800s, often without modern conveniences. She illustrated nearly one hundred books before her death at age ninety-two.

Presentation Suggestions

Arrange the characters in the following order: Narrator One, Narrator Two, Narrator Three, Starling Burgess, Rosamond Tudor, Tasha Tudor, Gwen, Thomas McCready, Bethany, Seth, and Tom. Characters can be dressed in clothing of the early 1900s if preferred.

Introductory and Follow-up Suggestions

Share books illustrated by Tasha Tudor. Then ask:

- Where do you think the illustrator got her ideas?

- What do you think it would be like to live on a farm?

- What do you think it would be like to live without running water or electricity?

After reading aloud the script, ask:

- If you could change your name, what would you call yourself?

- Tasha Tudor preferred living without many modern conveniences. What are the advantages of living a "simple life"?

- What are the disadvantages?

- What would you miss the most if you couldn't have electricity?

- What would you like best about a "simple life"?

Characters

Grade Two: Starling Burgess, Tom

Grade Three: Tasha Tudor, Gwen, Thomas McCready, Bethany, Seth

Grade Four: Narrator One, Narrator Two, Narrator Three, Rosamond Tudor

A Simple Life

Narrator One: Born in Boston in 1915, Tasha has an unusual childhood. Her father is named Starling Burgess. He designs yachts and airplanes. Her mother is named Rosamond Tudor. She keeps the name of Tudor when she gets married. She paints portraits.

Narrator Two: The nanny teaches Tasha how to cook and sew. Both parents love to read. They are not wealthy, but they have famous friends such as the writer Mark Twain. Tasha enjoys her pleasant childhood, even when it changes at age nine.

Rosamond Tudor: Tasha, your father and I need to talk with you about some changes.

Starling Burgess: You see, we are getting a divorce.

Rosamond Tudor: We won't be living together anymore. I'm moving to Greenwich Village, and I will keep painting.

Tasha Tudor: If you won't be living together, who will take care of me?

Starling Burgess: Now, you know that we love you very much, so we have given this a lot of thought. Greenwich Village is not the best place for a child. My work means that I can't take care of you.

Rosamond Tudor: My friend Gwen will take care of you during the week, and you'll spend weekends with me. So you'll have the country during the week and have the city on the weekends.

Tasha Tudor: I love her farm, but I'll miss both of you.

Narrator Three: Tasha loves the simple country life of Redding, Connecticut. She soon calls her mother's friend "Aunt Gwen" and makes many young friends. Gwen is creative and fun to be around.

From *Multi-Grade Readers Theatre: Picture Book Authors and Illustrators* by Suzanne I. Barchers and Charla R. Pfeffinger. Santa Barbara, CA: Teacher Ideas Press/Libraries Unlimited. Copyright © 2009.

Gwen: Tasha, I have written a new play for you and your friends. Why don't you gather them together and read through it?

Tasha Tudor: Can we use the clothes in the attic for our characters?

Gwen: Those should make great costumes. Just put them all away carefully when you're done.

Tasha Tudor: I love living here, Aunt Gwen, and when I grow up I want to have a farm, too.

Gwen: Tasha, if that is what you want to do, then I know you'll make it happen!

Narrator One: When Tasha is a teenager, her mother buys a farm near Gwen's. They spend the winters in Bermuda and summers on the farm. Tasha also discovers a love of art. She decides she wants to be an illustrator.

Narrator Two: Tasha grows up and falls in love with Thomas McCready. They get married in 1938, and Tasha dreams of having a farm.

Tasha Tudor: Thomas, do you think we can have our own farm? It doesn't need to be expensive or fancy. In fact, I'm looking forward to fixing it up myself.

Thomas McCready: I think we can get a farm someday. I also want you to think about something else.

Tasha Tudor: What do you mean?

Thomas McCready: I keep thinking about the story you wrote and illustrated for my niece. I think you should try to get it published.

Tasha Tudor: It's hard to break into publishing, but I could try.

Narrator Three: It takes a while to find a publisher for *Pumpkin Moonshine*. Tasha has two children and keeps dreaming of having a farm. Her royalties from a book of Mother Goose rhymes help her realize her dream.

Narrator One: Tasha and Thomas have two more children. Tasha works hard at improving the farm. They live without running water and electricity. She washes clothes by hand, gardens, bakes bread, and makes their clothes. The children fill their days with chores, playing, and helping Tasha with her illustrations.

From *Multi-Grade Readers Theatre: Picture Book Authors and Illustrators* by Suzanne I. Barchers and Charla R. Pfeffinger. Westport, CT: Teacher Ideas Press/Libraries Unlimited. Copyright © 2009.

Tasha Tudor: Children, put on these dress-up clothes so I can make some sketches.

Bethany: Can we have a tea party afterwards?

Tom: I'll only have a tea party if we can do a play, too.

Seth: We'll each be a prince, and you can be the pretty princess. We'll save you from a fire-breathing dragon.

Bethany: Will you read us a story when you're done painting, Mother?

Tasha Tudor: I'll read while you have your tea party, which might give you ideas for your play.

Tom: What story are you painting this time?

Seth: Are any of us in the story, Mother?

Tasha Tudor: You'll find out eventually. Let's get to work before we lose the afternoon light. After your tea party and play, you need to feed the horses, the cows, the chickens, the cats, the dogs. And don't forget to milk the cows!

Bethany, Seth, and Tom: *Mom!*

Narrator Two: Many of Tasha's stories do feature her children. She also creates stories about the children's dolls. The children don't mind taking care of the many farm animals and pets. Tasha makes life on the farm too much fun.

Narrator Three: After the children are grown up, Tasha moves to Vermont to be near Seth. He helps her build a big farmhouse, exactly as she likes it. She continues to live simply as she grows older.

Narrator One: When Tasha is in her early eighties, she talks about what it's like to get old.

Tasha Tudor: It's wonderful to grow old. . . . Everyone takes great care of you. . . . I fully believe old age is one of the most delightful periods of my life.

Narrator Two: Tasha Tudor is ninety-two when she dies of old age. She illustrated nearly one hundred books.

From *Multi-Grade Readers Theatre: Picture Book Authors and Illustrators* by Suzanne I. Barchers and Charla R. Pfeffinger. Santa Barbara, CA: Teacher Ideas Press/Libraries Unlimited. Copyright © 2009.

It Could Have Been Worse

Margot Zemach

1931–1989

Summary and Background Information

Margot Zemach was born in Hollywood, California. At age five she moved to New York when her mother, an actress, married Benjamin Zemach who was a dance and theatre director. Margot spent a lot of her time backstage on Broadway. She was fascinated with the transformation in actors from plain to characters on stage. As she waited backstage, she drew to keep herself amused. She also liked to tell jokes and stories to herself to keep from being bored. Finally, at age fifteen, she moved back to Hollywood. She received a Fulbright scholarship in art and went to Vienna, Austria, to study. While there, she met Harve Fischtom. They started writing books after their marriage. Harve did the words, Margot drew the illustrations. In 1968, they decided to take their three daughters to Europe, where they lived until Harve committed suicide in 1974. Margot then returned to California, where she lived and continued working with authors and writing books.

Presentation Suggestions

Narrators should sit off to one side of the staging. Hallie, Martha, and Gayla should be in the center with the other children arranged in a semicircle. Any number of readers can read Everyone's lines.

Introductory and Follow-up Suggestions

Using a map, show the children where Hollywood (Los Angeles), California, is. Trace Margot Zemach's travels from Hollywood to New York City, back to Hollywood, and then overseas. Point out the areas where she lived in Europe: Italy, Denmark, England, and Austria. Then ask:

- Margot lived in a lot of places. Which one do you think would be the most exciting?

- What is a folktale?

- What folktales do you know? How did you learn them?

After reading the script, ask:

- Margot and Harve used the name Zemach when they wrote their books. Their daughter, Kaethe, uses Zemach on her books, too. She says it is to carry on her mother's legacy. What do you think Margot's legacies are?

Characters

Grade Two: Mom, Rob, Erin

Grade Three: Hallie, Gayla, Martha, Everyone, Kelli, Wayne, Dottie, Jamie

Grade Four: Narrator One, Narrator Two

It Could Have Been Worse

Narrator One: Hallie, Martha, and Gayla have younger sisters and brothers. The girls want to do something fun with them during the summer.

Hallie: Mom? Martha, Gayla, and I want to do a play group this summer for the kids.

Mom: That is a great idea. Who are you going to invite?

Martha: We want to invite all the kids that live around us. They should be the same ages as Rob and Kelli.

Mom: Do you realize how many kids that is?

Gayla: We think there are twenty of them. They may not all come every time we do something.

Mom: What do you need from me, Hallie?

Hallie: First, can we use our backyard for the play group? And then would you fix lemonade and cookies for us?

Martha: You don't have to do the lemonade and cookies every week. My mother said she'd fix some, too.

Gayla: And my mom said she'd do cookies and lemonade.

Mom: How often are you going to have these play groups?

Hallie: We thought we'd do two each month until school starts. That would be six times.

Narrator Two: Hallie's mother agrees to have the play groups in their backyard. She also says she will make the cookies and lemonade for two of the days.

Narrator One: The girls make their invitations. They carefully plan what they will do each day. Finally, the first play day comes. Eighteen excited children gather in Hallie's backyard.

Mom: Girls, it looks like all the kids like your idea. What do you have planned for today?

From *Multi-Grade Readers Theatre: Picture Book Authors and Illustrators* by Suzanne I. Barchers and Charla R. Pfeffinger. Santa Barbara, CA: Teacher Ideas Press/Libraries Unlimited. Copyright © 2009.

Martha: Hallie's going to read *It Could Always Be Worse* by Margot Zemach. Then we'll see what things they can come up with for an *It Could Be Worse* game.

Gayla: After that we'll play tag so they have some exercise. Then we'll do lemonade and cookies. We thought we could sing some silly songs. That should fill the two hours.

Narrator Two: Hallie reads aloud *It Could Always Be Worse.* The girls have worked very hard on the questions for their game. They are going to use some of Margot's experiences for their questions. Martha explains the game to the kids and they start.

Hallie: When Margot was a little girl, she lived in New York. Her mother was an actress. She would spend her days backstage while her mother worked. She would draw pictures of all the actors she saw backstage.

Everyone: It could always be worse!

Martha: How could it be worse?

Rob: She could have lived in the country with no one around.

Kelli: She would only have trees and flowers to draw. Maybe she would see some insects, like flies and bumblebees.

Gayla: When she was fourteen years old, she moved back to Hollywood. She was born in Hollywood. She worked at a lot of odd jobs, but she failed at all of them. She decided to go to art school.

Everyone: It could always be worse!

Hallie: How could it be worse?

Wayne: She could have been good at one of those jobs. Then she would have never gone to art school or decided to illustrate a book.

Martha: At art school, she found out she enjoyed doing funny drawings. Sometimes she just used ink for line drawings. Other times she used watercolors to help tell the story.

Everyone: It could always be worse!

Gayla: How could it be worse?

Dottie: The pictures in her books would be really boring. They are a lot of fun to look at the way she drew them to make her stories better.

Hallie: Her husband wrote the words for the first book she illustrated. Then she retold folktales in most of her books. The book *It Could Always Be Worse* is a Yiddish folktale she retold.

Everyone: It could always be worse!

Martha: How could it be worse?

Jamie: We wouldn't get to hear a lot of folktales if she didn't retell them. My mother doesn't know any folktales.

Erin: Where do folktales come from?

Gayla: They come from all over the world. She and her husband and their daughters lived overseas for five years. She learned a lot of folktales while they lived there.

Rob: Then it *really* could have been worse. What if she had never gone over there to live?

Kelli: Did she write and illustrate only folktales?

Hallie: No. She did illustrations for *This Little Pig Went to Market* and other rhymes.

Martha: And she drew pictures for the song "Bingo."

Wayne: I love to sing that song. Can we sing it?

Gayla: We were going to sing it later this morning. We can sing it now if you wish.

Narrator One: Everyone around the block could hear the children singing. They had a lot of fun laughing at the mistakes they made while they sang.

Narrator Two: Finally, the morning is over. It is time for everyone to go home.

Jamie: This was a lot of fun. Thank you for asking us to come today.

Erin: I can't wait until we get to come back. What will we be doing next?

Hallie: We are going to keep that a surprise!

Gayla: Thanks for coming. We are glad you had a good time. Bye now.

Narrator One: The children leave, and Gayla, exhausted, looks at her friends.

Gayla: Well, everyone seemed to enjoy themselves. How do you think it went?

Hallie and Martha: It could have been worse!

Index of Authors and Illustrators

About the Authors

Suzanne I. Barchers, Ed.D., has written more than ninety books, ranging from college textbooks to children's books. (See books and other readers theatre scripts at www.storycart.com.) She has served as a public school teacher, an affiliate faculty for the University of Colorado, Denver, an acquisitions editor for Teacher Ideas Press, Managing Editor at *Weekly Reader,* and Editor in Chief and Vice President of LeapFrog Enterprises. She serves on the PBS Kids Media Advisory Board and is a member of the board of the Association of Educational Publishers (AEP).

Other recent titles from Suzanne include *Scary Readers Theatre*, *Multicultural Folktales*, *From Atalanta to Zeus: Readers Theatre from Greek Mythology, Classic Readers Theatre for Young Adults* (with Jennifer Kroll), *Judge for Yourself: Famous American Trials for Readers Theatre, Getting Ready to Read with Readers Theatre* (with Charla R. Pfeffinger), and *Against All Odds: Readers Theatre for Grades 3-8* (with Michael Ruscoe).

Charla R. Pfeffinger received her bachelor of science degree in elementary education and her master's degree in reading from Illinois State University, Normal, Illinois. Mrs. Pfeffinger was an educator in Illinois for twenty-two years before retiring. She has been a contributing author to *Learning* magazine, Storycart Press, and the author of *A Teen's Book of Lists, Holiday Readers Theatre,* and *Character Counts! Promoting Character Education: Readers Theatre.* She is co-author with Ms. Barchers on *Getting Ready to Read with Readers Theatre.*